# TECHNOLOGICAL IMPLICATIONS IN INDIAN INDUSTRIES

# TECHNOLOGICAL IMPLICATIONS IN INDIAN INDUSTRIES

**P. Dhiraviyam**

**ABHIJEET PUBLICATIONS**

**DELHI 110094**

**ABHIJEET PUBLICATIONS**
2/46 Tukhmeerpur Extension
Delhi-110 094
Phone: 011-22960492, 65698474
E-mail: abhijeetpublication@gmail.com

TECHNOLOGICAL IMPLICATIONS IN INDIAN INDUSTRIES

*First Published 2008*



ISBN 978-81-89886-83-7



PRINTED IN INDIA

Published by J.K. Singh for Abhijeet Publications, Delhi-110 094, Lasertypeset by Gaurav Graphics, New Delhi and Printed at Himanshu Printers, Delhi.

Dedicated to my Parents

**A. Palaniyappa Pillai**
and
**Vamboyeammal**

# Preface

After the Introduction of New economic policy in India our Indian Industries has underwent radical changes. Because of the new technology and innovative methods and means of production helps us to update our technical know-how our Indian manufacturing industries have registered a remarkable rate of progress in recent times. This book makes an attempt to throw light on the structural adjustment among the various industries and some technological modifications.

This book is a synoptic look on technological implications, and I should not claim it covers all aspects of technological development. Suggestions for improvement are always welcome.

To thank profusely scholars and authorities is a pleasure indeed.

I am greatly indebted to Dr. A. Arunachalam, M.A., M.Phil., M.L., Ph.D., M.B.A., Chairman and Correspondent of Adaikalamatha College, Vallam Thanjore.

I owe my sincere thanks to respected Principal Dr. R. Kathian, M.Com., M.Phil., Ph.D., for his timely help.

I am thankful to Abhijeet Publications, New Delhi for their interest and co-operation in publishing this book.

I do not claim that could cover all the aspects of the TECHNOLOGICAL IMPLICATION IN INDIAN INDUSTRIES within the limited space, but I firmly believe that this book well be very useful to all concerned.

**Prof. P. Dhiraviyam**
Vallam
May 2008

# Contents

# 1

# *Technological Implications of Structural Adjustment*

## Technological Scene on Eve of Structural Adjustment

With the benefit of hindsight, we can see four major periods in the evolution of industrial and technological policies of the Indian state, each period defined by departures from some of the positions taken in the previous period. The first period, 1950-1965, was marked by the state acquiring and keeping the lead in the producer goods sector, i.e., capital goods and some key intermediate goods, leaving almost the entire consumer goods and the non-strategic parts of the intermediate goods sectors to private Indian and foreign capital. During the second period, 1966-1984, the emphasis on state ownership and control of the strategic parts of Indian industry gradually declined, and the strategy of self-reliantly catching up with the west technologically was abandoned in practice (though not in rhetoric). The third period, which spans the years

1985-1991, signalled the retreat of the state from the 'commanding heights of the economy'. It initiated the entry of the private sector into areas formerly reserved exclusively for the public sector. It also witnessed a strengthening of the strategy of 'import liberalisation for modernisation of industry' which was set in motion already during the latter half of the second period. The onset of the so-called 'stabilisation and structural adjustment programme' in July 1991 heralds the start of the fourth period. (For a detailed presentation of the Indian government's industrial policies over the last 40 years, the reader is referred to Sandesara 1992.)

The conventional division of India's so-called 'mixed economy' into 'public' and 'private' sectors can be misleading. They are two sides of the same coin. It should be borne in mind that from independence (1947) onwards the strategic aim of those who wielded real (as opposed to nominal) power was to make India into a strong nation-state on the foundations of a strong capitalist economy. There was a convergence of views between the state and domestic private capital as to their respective roles in this endeavour: the state would provide highly subsidised transport, communication and social infrastructure, as well as basic materials and energy (e.g., steel, chemicals, coal and electricity) required by industry (both private and public) create highly protected domestic markets for the output of domestic industry; the private sector would accumulate capital and grow by supplying the domestic market for consumer goods. State intervention on behalf of domestic industry has been and will continue to be the key issue in the process of successfully industrialising any country, let alone India, as the literature on the economic development of Europe,

North America and east Asia repeatedly demonstrates. (See the critique of the World Bank's 1993 report on 'The East Asian Miracle' in the special section of World Development, April 1994.) The question, then, is not whether the state should intervene, but how and how much. As a background to the analysis in this paper of how structural adjustment is likely to affect industry and technology in India, we will in this section briefly review the technological outcome of the state intervention practised over the last four decades.

During the first policy period (1950-1965), with its three first five-year plans single-mindedly concentrating on building domestic manufacturing capacity in capital goods, India had strong technical collaboration with both the west and the erstwhile communist bloc. But with the onset of the second policy period in the mid-1960s, technology transfer from the communist bloc began to decline in favour of increasing collaboration with western transnational corporations. By the mid-1980s, when the third policy period with its strong bias towards liberalisation had been ushered in, the former Soviet Union and eastern Europe were out of the picture altogether. Already by then, technology agreements with the OECD region were running into several thousands. Since then, the demand for, and the approval of, technology agreements have greatly accelerated, as is evident if we note that during 1985-1990 the total number of new agreements approved were 5,203, which was 80 per cent more than the 2,916 approval over the preceding five-year period 1980-1984 [India-DSIR 1992]. These figures bear eloquent witness to the fruition of the quiet and implicit policy embarked upon in the early 1970s of abandoning the quest for self-reliant indigenous technological development. Official industrial statistics in India are now graced by a new concept of classification, the 'foreign collaborated firm', as in Wipro-Sun, HPL-HP, PSI-Bull, etc. [Vyasulu 1993].

Let us now turn to the question of what actually has been achieved on the basis of this massive import of technology.

## Analytical Framework

The concept of modern technology we adopt is a broad one. Its 'embodied' or 'hardware' form consists of tools, machinery, equipment and vehicles, which together make up the category of capital goods. Its 'disembodied' or 'software' form encompasses the knowledge and skills required for the use, maintenance, repair, production, adaptation and innovation of capital goods, which are often also labelled in the literature as 'the know-how and the know-why of processes and products'. In our usage, knowledge and skills refer not only to scientific, engineering and technical abilities, but also to the skills associated with organisation, management and information. Hereafter we use the terms 'knowledge' and 'skills' interchangeably.

We find it analytically useful to classify modern technology into two broad types, standard-modern and highly-modern, on the basis of five indicators: automation, science-relatedness, research-intensity, dominant innovative skills and leading sectors [Freeman 1974]. These two broad types, which we hereafter denote by 'standard-tech' and 'high tech', are characterised respectively by 'medium' and 'high' values in their degrees of automation, science-relatedness and research intensity. For a detailed exposition of this approach to technology analysis the reader is referred to Bhagavan (1990). The range of professional skills required for the regular use, maintenance, repair and production of the capital goods belonging to these two types of technologies depends of course on the specific industrial and infrastructural branches at which one is looking In general, they comprise a large number, but not all, of the skill categories listed under the International Standard Classification of Occupations, excluding those that come under sales, services and agriculture.

A country's capacity to innovate in standard and high techs presupposes the existence of a good base in the skills mentioned above. However, that is not enough. In addition, one has to acquire capacity in certain areas which are specifically innovation-oriented. Research scientists and research engineers represent the class of people with leading innovative skills. For much of the century-long duration of the standard modern era in the west (1860-1960), the research scientist and the research engineer worked individualistically without being tied to 'systems approaches'. The transition from standard to high tech, both in 'old' products (say, textile machinery) and in entirely new ones (say, digital telecommunication), depends crucially on systems approaches to solving problems. The innovations associated with the high tech area, and with the transition from standard to high tech in already known products, appear impossible without professionalised R and D entities in which research scientists and engineers, as well as system and symbol analysts, work as teams.

Roughly speaking, the transition from the standard-modern to the highly-modern era began in western

Europe and north America in the 1960s. Some examples of the leading sectors that exemplify standard-tech capital goods and skills are steel, railways, electricals, automobiles, plastics, synthetic textile, and synthetic dyes. However, all these 'old' products have made the transition and are now available in their high tech avatars. Examples of entirely new leading sectors that have arisen with high tech are microelectronics, computers, digital and satellite-based telecommunications, robotics, informatics, biotechnology (based on genetic engineering) and new materials.

### Using and Replicating Imported Standard-Modern Technology

In the following we summarise the factors and measures that helped India acquire, within a space of 30 years (1950-1980), the capacity to use and replicate a great variety of imported standard-modern capital goods, as well as a few highly-modern ones. However, what has signally failed is the apparent effort to acquire the capacity to design and innovate new standard-tech, let alone the very much more complex high tech. On paper, of course, the Indian state formulated a host of measures to generate this capacity. But no serious efforts were made to systematically enforce these measures and to create the environment that would oblige both the public and private sectors, as well as government-funded R and D establishments, to undertake technology designing and technology innovation.

Table 1 shows that imports of consumer goods had been drastically reduced already by the early 1970s in comparison With the other two sectors. By then India was meeting most of domestic demand for consumer goods by domestic production, importing mainly a small range of consumer durables for its high-income stratum that it was not yet making itself.

Machinery dominated the import composition of capital goods, accounting for nearly 90 per cent by 1981. The average annual growth rates of imports of machinery and transport equipment were also very high right to the end of the 1970s, reaching nearly 17 per cent by 1980.

Since, by the early 1980s, India had achieved a large capacity in domestic manufacture of capital goods, the question arises as to why imports of capital goods did not decline much from the 1970s level. The answer lies in the fact that although India had achieved near self-sufficiency in replicating standard-tech by the late 1970s, it was very far from doing that in high tech, on which was what the capital goods imports in the 1980s and beyond concentrated. Nearly 30 per cent of the capital goods imports in the early 1980s consisted of high tech such as electrical power machinery and switch gear, telecommunication equipment, computers, aircraft and ships [Bhagavan 1990]. In comparing the monetary values of imports, one should remember that the cost of even one high tech capital good, say,. a long-range civilian jet aircraft, may be several orders of magnitudes higher than that of a large number of consumer durables, say, dishwashers.

India began exporting standard-tech capital goods from the late 1970s onwards, accounting by 1984 for 10 per cent of total value of exports [Lall 1990].

## Skill Structure of Workforce

One of the key indicators of a country's technological level is the skill composition of its workforce. The historical pattern is that employment in modern industry and infrastructure overtakes that in agriculture, as a country becomes more industrialised. And since substantial parts of industrial and infrastructural work require machine-related skills, a relative increase in industrial and infrastructural employment can be taken to be a rough and ready indicator of an increase in the skill level of the workforce.

Looking at Table 2 we note that South Korea conforms to this pattern, but not India. Between 1970 and 1989, there was a massive shift downwards in agriculture's share of employment in South Korea by 30 percentage points (category 6), accompanied by a shift upwards in the share of industry and infrastructure by 12 percentage points (categories 7, 8 and 9). In India, there has been no shift at all in industry's and infrastructure's share of employment over the period 1971-1981. It is immobile at 13 per cent, while that in agriculture has decreased by more than six percentage points. That decrease is in effect a corresponding rise in unemployment, as the other sectors have also stayed motionless, as is clear from Table 2. Although the Indian data refer to 1981, the well-documented fact that there has been virtually no growth in employment in the organised registered sector of industry during the 1980s [Ghose 1993] let us infer that industry's and infrastructure's share of total employment in the early 1990s is very likely to be less than it was in the early 1980s. Thus, at a very aggregate level, we can venture the opinion that there has been no structural shift within the Indian workforce in the direction of increasing total machine-related skill content.

Professional, technical and managerial personnel are of strategic importance in industrial and technological advance. Here too, India seems not to have undergone the kind of structural change that rapid technological progress requires. The figures for categories 1 and 2 in Table 2 demonstrate that over the 10-year period 1971-1981 these two categories stood structurally still at 3.6 per cent of the total workforce. There is no factor in the Indian economy that indicates that this figure may have moved up in the 1980s. Rather, the opposite is true. The measure of Indian non-performance becomes clear when compared with South Korea's strong shift towards higher skills as revealed by the four percentage point increase in categories 1 and 2 over the period 1970-1989.

### Scientific and Technological Manpower

Under the strategy of relatively rapid industrialisation that India adopted after independence, there arose a sharply increasing demand for large numbers of literate workers skilled in basic industrial skills. The tradition of recruiting unskilled (and most often illiterate) labourers, and training them on the job to acquire the skills that any particular enterprise required, proved wholly inadequate. It was argued that the expanding secondary education system would meet this challenge.

**Table 1: Structure of Imports of Manufactured Goods: Percentage Distribution of Value of Imports by Broad Sectors**

| *Year* | *Capital Goods* | *Intermediate Goods* | *Consumer Goods* |
|---|---|---|---|
| 1970 | 16.7 | 73.6 | 6.8 |
| 1981 | 13.4 | 77.5 | 9.1 |

*Sources:* United Nations Yearbook of International Trade Statistics, various issues.

On an average, about 1 5 per cent of the employees in industry and infrastructure belong to the skilled category. In theory, the supply of recruits into this group should therefore be easily ensurable by Indian secondary schools even at their current very low proportional intakes. One may be tempted to conclude that the supply of recruits for skilled work does not pose a problem in India. However, industrial employers would, in the first instance, be looking for vocationally trained candidates rather than fresh secondary school leavers. Therefore a better measure of the actual recruiting base would be the output of vocational schools that train pupils over several years in one or more industrial skills.

In the early 1980s, India was producing around 4,00,000 vocational school leavers per year, which was roughly 7 per cent of employment in manufacturing. This should be compared with South Korea's 8,40,000, corresponding to 40 per cent of manufacturing jobs [Lall 1990]. As mentioned earlier, the 1980s in India were the years of 'jobless growth'. So in terms of absorptive capacity, even the very modest output by Indian vocational schools (in comparison with South Korea's absolute figures, let alone on a per capita basis) was already too high for Indian industry.

Technicians take a midway position between skilled workers and graduate scientists and engineers. Their role is crucial in industrial development. Ideally, their work should consist of diagnosing and putting right major faults in a range of sophisticated designing and engineering sections, leaving the actual implementation of the designs to skilled workers. However, in the absence of any significant design work in Indian industry at present, the technical-liaising dimension has remained dormant. Instead, technicians' present primary duties are as foremen and supervisors, exercising technical and social control over factory floor labour. In other words, the talents and training of technicians are being underutilised.

One among several illustrations of the telling contrasts in skill levels and skill use between sluggish and dynamic industrial sectors is provided by the figures for technicians in India and South Korea. From Table 3 one can see that whereas there were more than 50,000 technicians per million of the population in South Korea as early as 1981, there were less than 800 technicians per million of the population in India as late as 1990. But when it comes to the production of graduate scientists and engineers, the Indian figures are roughly at par with South Korea's, at around 3,000 per million of the total population (Table 3). The two countries are also at par in proportional enrolment in higher education and specifically in science and engineering (Tables 4 and 5).

### Inverted Educational Pyramid

The Indian performance in enrolment in secondary education is very poor, not least when compared to the leaders among the late industrialisers like South Korea. It is seen from Table 4 that by the mid-1980s while South Korea was approaching near universal secondary education, India had not even managed to get halfway to that goal.

In the debate about the role of human resources in development, it is now increasingly acknowledged that without universal primary and secondary education it is not possible to generate the process of self-sustaining development. With universal secondary education, every child approaching adulthood will have internalised the primary knowledge base and the basic techniques of learning, with which she can acquire a whole range of new knowledge and skills. It is not a coincidence that the OECD countries and the dynamic east Asian economies (of which South Korea is used here as a reference example to compare and contrast with India) first concentrated on attaining universal secondary education, before making higher education more widely accessible. In terms of financial resources, India has done the opposite: It has poured more public money into higher education on a proportional basis than into primary and secondary education. It shares this feature of the "inverted educational pyramid" with many other developing countries [Upendranath 1993a]. But now with the SAP there are firm indications that this lopsided behaviour will be put right and primary and secondary education budget.

The imperatives that lie behind this skewed policy of promoting higher education while grossly neglecting primary and secondary education are those of the politically powerful middle class [Upendranath 1993a]. It wants higher education for its offspring partly for reasons of social status and partly because it is the minimum qualification required for any white collar job. But the contradiction of supplying degrees in excess of the needs of a sluggish economy has been transparent for a long time in the guise of graduate unemployment. It is reported that about 1.2 million science and engineering graduates and technicians were registered as unemployed in 1990.

The difference between quantity and quality is nowhere more apparent than in the realms of the work done by scientists, engineers and technicians. For instance, although India is reputed to have the world's third largest combined stock of these three professions, its industrial productivity has still recently been negative and the quality of its industrial products open to serious misgiving. These negative outcomes have their origins in the following conditions under which higher education has been, and continues to be, conducted. First, and perhaps the most devastating, is that non-academic, non-merit factors are decisive in gaining entry into professional courses. Second is the predominantly book-bound orientation of the training, with rote-learning and exams-passing almost totally displacing problem-solving approaches. Third, out of the countless number of universities and colleges, only a tiny fraction has the resources to provide basic laboratories and workshops to back up theoretical work—for the others with no experimental facilities, science simply becomes theology. Fourth, with higher education having exploded in numbers beyond imagination, there simply are not enough places in industries and other professional sectors to place undergraduates for short periods of practical training. On top of all this, there is the annual brain drain of promising young talent to technologically greener pastures elsewhere. To quote from the *Far Eastern Economic Review* (1992): "Out of the 190 recognised universities, the world-class science and engineering institutions number only about a dozen. These schools turn out 2,000-3,000 graduates a year. About a third opt for management careers or the civil service. Another third emigrate to the US, Canada and Singapore."

## INDIAN R AND D: NOT TECHNOLOGY INNOVATION, BUT TECHNOLOGY ABSORPTION

The explicit involvement of the government of India in funding targeted scientific and industrial research predates independence in 1947. In 1942, following the British model, the then colonial government in New Delhi established a Council of Scientific and Industrial Research (CSIR) to oversee and be in charge of a few national laboratories, created at that time to investigate whether imported industrial raw materials could be replaced by local ones to overcome the problems created by the ongoing Second World War. Recognising the central importance of technology to economic development, the government of independent India rapidly expanded the number of national research laboratories and institutes under the CSIR umbrella to over 40 by the late 1960s. They were spread over major cities in the country and covered a wide field in the natural and engineering sciences. Their mandate was to do both 'pure' and 'applied' research, and in particular to address the technological problems of industry and contribute to technological innovation. Since then, the exercise has been repeated in other fields like agriculture, forestry, marine resources, medicine, electronics and biotechnology, with each new area being placed under a separate ministerial department that funds and controls the corresponding national laboratories and institutes.

**Government Research Laboratories**

Total R and D funding in India grew very rapidly during the 1980s, increasing by nearly a factor of six over the period 1981-1991, from slightly over Rs 7 billion in 1981 to Rs 42 billion in 1991 (US $ 2.3 billion at the then exchange rate). Eighty per cent of the 1991 funding was spent in government labs and public sector enterprises, with the private sector accounting for the remaining 20 per cent (India-DST 1992). Over half of the government funding, Rs 18 billion, went to three organisations: the Defence Research and Development Organisation (with its huge number of R and D units), the department of atomic energy and the department of space research.

In order to ensure that top class engineers would be available for leading industrial development work, the Indian government, with generous financial and technical assistance from the west, created five Indian Institutes of Technology (IITs). Like the national labs, they too were geographically spread out, with two in the north and one each in east, south and west. Besides providing undergraduate and postgraduate education in the engineering sciences, they were charged with the responsibility of being in the forefront of technological research.

The third approach to promoting technological research was much more diffuse. It was to try and coax both public and private sector industries into establishing in-house R and D units with import tax rebates and generous amortisation rates for R and D equipment.

The scientific establishment in India routinely bemoans the fact that India spends less than its role models in east Asia on R and D as a proportion of its total GDP. For instance, in 1990, Japan, South Korea, Taiwan and India spent, respectively, US $ 85.6 billion (2.98 per cent of GDP), 3.2 billion (1.83 per cent) 2 billion (1.41 per cent) and 2.5 billion (0.88 per cent) on R and D. What they conveniently forget to mention is that the overwhelming part of east Asian funding comes from the domestic private sector, which really makes sure that it gets value for its money [Sigurdson 1990].

A corollary of this is the stunning performance of the east Asians in making technical changes, in generating technological innovations and putting new products and processes on the market. Considering the truly colossal sums spent on civilian R and D by the government over the last four decades, India has little to show in terms of civilian innovation that is its own. From toothbrushes to tractors. From shoe polish to ships, from bicycles to buses, any improvements that the Indian customer may have enjoyed are still the result of continuing import of technology. The Indian customer is also unaware of any incremental technical improvement in commodities of regular use that government-funded R and D may have hit upon. Not that private sector R and D has done any better.

What ever else they may have been accomplished, it is now clear that the government research labs and institutes have been less than marginal in promoting technical change and innovation in Indian industry and infrastructure. The labs charge industry with deliberately ignoring their contributions in preference to imported technology. Industry claims that the labs have concentrated on work which is of no relevance to industry. The accusations fly back and forth. What the verdict of the present Indian government is can be inferred from the fact that it imparted a sharp shock to the government research labs and institutes in 1992 by not approving the expected automatic annual increase in their budget allocation, hinting that the future would be pretty dire. The ministry of finance has told them to generate 30 per cent of their budget from commissioned work from the private sector. At the time of writing, several of them have set up marketing units and task forces to try and sell their know-how to private industry.

A recent empirical study into industrial R and D in India [Alam 1993] finds that "a large number of firms were unhappy with their experiences with these [government] laboratories and institutes. Most felt that the facilities available with these institutes were adequate, but that their approach to research for industry was not very positive. The most common feeling was that the national laboratories and research institutes were not used to commercial culture and did not appreciate the importance of completing jobs on time. This has led to frustration and losses for the firms. Firms also felt that the facilities available with these laboratories are grossly under utilised and could be used by industry for testing prototypes, etc".

The IITs seem to have fared somewhat better than the CSIR labs in responding to industry's needs. To quote from the same report [Alam 1993 ]: "Our case studies reveal that ...industry sponsored research projects (at the IITs) aimed at solving specific problems". Be that as it may, of the original two-part intention that the IITs should not only produce the very best engineering graduates but also retain the intellectually brightest of them to do technological R and D within the country, only the first appears to have been seriously tried. Apparently about a thousand IIT graduates leave India each year for North America.

## In-House R and D in Industrial Firms

That brings us to a consideration of in-house R and D in industry. A look at the macro-statistics gathered and annually published by the Indian government tells us that the number of industrial firms with some kind of in-house R and D has been steadily increasing over the last two decades and is now nearing the figure 1200. It also tells us that the total amount spent by them on R and D as a proportion of their total sales is about 0.66 per cent, averaged over the six-year period 1985-1990 [India-DST 1992]. Considerable amounts of case study material and analyses, at both the micro and macro levels, are now available on why Indian industrial firms, both public and private, invest in R and D and what fruit that investment has borne. We summarise below the main findings of a number of these studies [Alam 1993; Desai 1988, 1990; Gumaste 1988; Kathuria 1989; Katrak 1989; Kumar 1987; Lall 1987; Tyabji 1993], which also investigate the effect of government policy on promoting R and D at the firm level.

| *Country/Year* | *ISCO Major Groups (see notes below) Percentages* | | | | | | |
|---|---|---|---|---|---|---|---|
| | *1* | *2* | *3* | *4* | *5* | *6* | *7/8/9* |
| India 1971 | 2.7 | 0.9 | 2.8 | 4.0 | 3.3 | 72.5 | 12.9 |
| 1981 | 2.7 | 0.9 | 2.8 | 3.9 | 2.6 | 66.1 | 13.0 |
| S. Korea 1970 | 3.1 | 0.9 | 5.8 | 9.9 | 6.5 | 49.6 | 21.2 |
| 1989 | 6.7 | 1.4 | 12.1 | 14.3 | 10.5 | 18.8 | 33.6 |

*Notes:*

1. The above percentages do not always add up to 100, because we have excluded from (he table the categories 'workers not classifiable by occupation' and 'unemployed'.
2. For India, 1981 is the latest year for which published data were available in United Nations sources at the time of writing.
3. By 'workforce' we mean those categorised as 'economically active population' by the UN Statistical Office.
4. 1 = Professional, technical and related workers
   2 = Administrative and managerial workers
   3 = Clerical and related workers
   4 = Sales workers
   5 = Service workers
   6 = Agriculture, animal husbandry and related workers
   7/8/9 = Production and related workers, transport equipment and labourers.

*Sources:* ILO, Yearbook of Labour Statistics, 1990 and 1991.

Empirical studies of several hundred firms were conducted by some of the above-mentioned authors. They covered the fields of ceramics, electronics, electricals, machinery, automobiles, metallurgy, metal working, chemical engineering, minerals and mining, paper, textiles, leather and food processing. The firms identified the following activities as the principal objectives of their R and D work: product adaptation, product diversification, indigenisation of components, indigenisation of raw materials and testing. Of these, the first three were mentioned the most often. Some firms also claimed that they did some 'product development'. On a closer look, what this claim boiled down to is minor modifications of imported articles, or their imitation or an expansion of the product line by introducing new imports.

One of the measures that the government insisted on being implemented within foreign technology agreements was the rapid replacement of imported part-components by locally manufactured ones. This process of 'indigenisation' of component manufacture, as it has come to be called, also required rapid absorption of increasing volumes of foreign technology. The R and D units became the principal vehicles for indigenisation. On analysing their data, the authors find that the primary objective of firms in setting up R and D units was to develop in-house skills to understand how the imported capital goods function (know-how), why they do what they do (know-why), what their strengths and weaknesses are, and what the critical points are of which one has to be aware. This process is called 'technology absorption'.

It is very important to note that technological innovation, which among other things involves acquisition of design capacity, does not feature among the R and D goals of the firms studied. Product adaptation, which usually involves some incremental technical change, is the first step towards product innovation. With most of the attention being focused on absorbing the know-how, the learning of know-why receded into the background. Without know-why it is not possible to successfully attempt change and adaptation in imported technology to suit local conditions. Nor was such change the first priority of most firm owners. Improvement in product quality, production efficiency and labour productivity were of much more central concern; these could be tackled on the basis of the know-how that came with the imported technology.

Firms in electronics and electricals spend more on R and D as a percentage of sales than other firms, with metal industries spending least, while machinery and chemicals take intermediate positions. Roughly the same pattern holds for royalty and other payments for dis-embodied technology (i.e., technological knowledge) as a proportion of sales. A plausible hypothesis that would explain both these patterns is that the rate of technical change in electronics and electricals is much higher than in other areas, leading to frequent imports of new technology, which in turn necessitates a continuous strengthening of the firm's technology absorption capability.

A sharp increase has been noted in the total volume of payments made for foreign technical knowledge (disembodied technology). But, at the same time the case studies find, somewhat to their surprise, that the more generous terms allowed for payments for technological knowledge since 1985 and 1991 have not led to any significant increases in the import of technological knowledge by individual firms as individual firms. The increase in the total volume of payments would then mean that substantial numbers of new firms have entered the market as knowledge buyers. A prime reason why the costs of individual agreements have not risen to the degree expected is that firms are buying only very specific bits of hardware and software, and not a whole composite machinery. This ability to 'un package' technology and buy only that which cannot be locally generated is a promising sign of the growing industrial maturity of the country.

It seems as though the limiting factor on R and D investment was not the terms set by the government but quite simply the level of the financial resources available to firms. In fact, most case studies underline the fact that on an average an Indian firm spends far too little on knowledge import and in-house R and D to really be able to attempt technological innovation. The firms are fully aware of this limitation. Their purpose in establishing in-house R and D is first and foremost to absorb technology. One of India's leading industrialists is quoted as saying that "none of this [i. e., in-house R and D] is research. It's mostly reverse engineering. Basic research would mean a lot of time reinventing the wheel, and the funds required are such that most Indian companies can't compete—Honda's R and D expenditure is more than my annual turnover" [*Far Eastern Economic Review,* 1992].

Firms point out that a technology agreement makes it easier to source the capital goods and production inputs through the foreign partner's knowledge of, and contacts in, the supplying market. Indian firms usually do not have the resources to build-up such information and market capabilities. In other words, technology agreements are often even less significant than they are made out to be—they are less the vehicles for upgrading technological knowledge than a practical and relatively inexpensive way of sourcing capital goods and inputs. An extreme is reached when, as in some leather and textile firms, the foreign collaboration agreement is nothing more than a means of obtaining market intelligence. Analyses of macro-policy factors that promoted or inhibited R and D activities at firm level revealed the following trends. The smallness of the size of most Indian firms in comparison with those in the OECD region in an inhibiting factor when it comes to significant investments in R and D. In contrast to that, firms' export capacity and market competitiveness had no significant impact in either direction. The more liberal rules introduced in 1985 and 1991 for foreign equity holdings in Indian firms, as well as for import of technology, seem to have started eroding the earlier rationale for investing in R and D. However, it was also noted that firms which increased their import of technology and production inputs also invested more in R and D to generate the appropriate kinds and levels of technology absorption capacity.

## Imposition of Stabilisation and Structural Adjustment Programme

The liberalisation of imports and foreign exchange transactions, sanctioned by the 1985 policies, ate rapidly into India's foreign exchange reserves. The sudden increase in the import bill of oil caused by the Gulf war, though brief, was another severe drain. In the aftermath of the Gulf war, forex remittances from Indian workers from the Gulf states dried up. With the confidence in the Indian economy declining, Indian residents abroad began withdrawing their forex deposits from Indian banks. By the summer of 1991 the forex reserves were down to a level insufficient even to cover essential imports for a few weeks!

The total external debt had meanwhile climbed to 70billion US dollars, corresponding to nearly a quarter of the total GDP, giving India the dubious distinction of being the third largest debtor nation in the third world after Brazil and Mexico. With the forex reserves at rock bottom, India found itself for the first time in the position of having to default on its debt servicing which had now climbed to 22 per cent of export income, a move that would have choked off all future avenues for foreign loan and credit facilities. Five years after the optimistic projections made by the Indian government in 1985 while launching its liberalisation policies, its fiscal crisis had not got any better, but worse. A measure of that crisis is the fact that the accumulated domestic borrowing of the Indian government (financed largely out of the savings of middle class households held in banks, bonds and sundry financial institutions and instruments) had reached a staggering 55 per cent of the GDP by 1991. In the same year, consumer price inflation had risen to 14 per cent from the 8 per cent in 1985.

The balance of payments crisis and the fiscal crisis of the state are deeply structural and cannot be resolved by short-term measures. But a quick short-term 'fix' had to be found to stave off impending disaster, and it came in the shape of yet another massive loan from the International Monetary Fund. But that loan was conditional on the Indian government's commitment to implementing the IMF's standard prescription of Stabilisation and Structural Adjustment (SSAP). This is not the place to recount the details of the measures proposed within the SSAP for various sectors of the Indian economy and society. For a meticulous, if somewhat positivist, summary that captures the essentials, the reader is referred to Das (1993).

The thrust of the stabilisation policies is to devalue the currency to make exports cheaper and imports dearer, to check inflation through a squeeze on money supply, credits, wages and incomes, and to stimulate investment and demand through tax reductions. The principal long-term aims of the structural adjustment programme (SAP) are to reshape the economy along 'free market' lines which would drastically curtail the role of the state in the ownership and control of economic assets and activities, give the private sector (both domestic and foreign) the dominant role in all sectors of the economy, promote unimpeded imports of foreign goods, services, investment and technology, provide special incentives to promote exports, end all subsidies and sharply reduce state financing of social services such as education, health and transport.

A vigorous debate is taking place among Indian academics, policy-makers and government officials on the pros and cons of the SAP. A great deal has been written and published. To obtain a quick overview of the positions taken, the reader is referred to ILO-ARTEP (1992), Raghuram (1991), Gupta (1993) and Nayyar (1993).

To sum up, then, 'liberalisation' and the SAP were not bolts from the blue. Between the 'closing' of the economy in the early 1950s and its near total 'opening' in the early 1990s, "one can discern a gradual political-economic process, the turn towards the 'opening' already being taken by the mid-1970s. The fiscal crisis of the state and the balance of payments crisis, which came to a head in 1991, are but the latest episodes in a long drawn out struggle between the main contenders for economic and political power" [Bardhan 1984; Patnaik 1986; Kurien 1986; Bhagavan 1987].

## New Industrial and Technological Policies Under SAP

The new industrial policy introduced by the Indian government as part of the SAP extends and completes the liberalisation measures of 1985. We summarise its main features and the associated technological measures below:

(a) The licensing system has been abolished for all branches of mining and manufacturing industry except those involving strategic and security concerns, social and environmental concerns, hazardous chemicals and elite consumer durables. These exceptions comprise the following: defence, aerospace, explosives and fossil fuels; alcohol, tobacco and asbestos; sugar, animal fats and oils; leather, furs and skins; chemically treated wood products, paper and newsprint; pharmaceutical; motor cars, entertainment electronics and household white goods (refrigerators, washing machines, air-conditioners, etc). The small-scale sector would, however, be automatically exempt from licensing for any of the above 18 branches which fall within the list of commodities already exclusively reserved for it through earlier policies. The upper limit on investment in plant and machinery has been raised from Rs 3.5 million to Rs 6 million for small-scale units in general, and to 7 million for so-called ancillary units of bigger firms and for export-oriented small-scale firms. Other firms can now hold up to a quarter of the total investment in any small-scale unit. No licensing is required for expansion of existing production capacities, or for adding new product lines within the existing commodity area of the firm (so-called broad-banding).

(b) Permission to import capital goods would be automatic for projects which ensure foreign exchange through foreign investment, provided their GIF value is less than 25 per cent of the total value of the plant and equipment, subject to a ceiling of Rs 20 million.

(c) A virtual 'open door' policy for foreign investment, with an upper limit of 51 per cent of the equity in any given firm, comes into effect in 34 so-called 'high priority industries', which covers a great many major branches in capital, intermediate and consumer goods sectors, as well as in tourism. To quality for such automatic clearance, the foreign exchange cost of the imported capital goods must be covered by the foreign equity.

(d) Technology agreements with foreign suppliers would be automatically approved for the above-mentioned 34 high priority industries, subject to upper limits of Rs 10 million for lump sum payments and 8 per cent of sales for royalty payments. These payments, for which foreign exchange would be automatically approved, would last for a maximum of 10 years from the date of agreement, or seven years after the commencement of production. Non-priority industries would also enjoy this privilege of automatic approval provided they did not claim the same 'free' access to foreign exchange technology payments to which the priority industries have a right.

(e) No permission would be required for hiring foreign technical personnel.

(f) The eight industries hitherto reserved exclusively for the public sector would now be open to the private sector. They are defence; atomic energy and associated fuels and materials' fossil fuels; the mining of ferrous and non-ferrous ores, as well as some strategic and precious metals; and railway transport.

(g) Public sector firms would be subjected to critical review, which would not exclude the possibilities of closure, liquidation, rehabilitation or privatisation. The criteria that would guide any action in these directions would be related to inefficiency in performance, low levels in technology, smallness of scale, low social priority, and not least the existence of well-developed private sector capacities supplying the same commodities. The government has announced its intention to sell 20 per cent of its holdings in the public sector, while simultaneously directing public sector firms to generate more internal resources. Public sector firms would from now on be held to agreed levels of performance through binding memoranda of understanding. Their boards would be made more professional and autonomous and given greater power.

(h) The central provisions of the Monopolies and Restrictive Trade Practices (MRTP) Act have been scrapped. Mergers and takeovers are now freely permitted. Prior government approval for expanding present undertakings or for starting new ones is no longer necessary.

(i) Both imports and exports have been greatly liberalised. Only very few commodities are banned outright from import and export, while between 60 and 70 are placed on the restricted list for exports and imports respectively. Capital goods are being particularly favoured both with easier import rules for a great majority of items and enhance incentives for their exports.

**Table 3: Scientific and Technical Manpower (Employed)**

| *Country* | *Year* | *Scientists + Engineers* | | *Technicians* | |
|---|---|---|---|---|---|
| | | *No (000)* | *Per mn Pop* | *No (000)* | *Per mn Pop* |
| India | 1990 | 2471 | 2995 | 639 | 774 |
| South Korea | 1981 | 94 | 2478 | 1931 | 50828 |

*Source:* UNESCO, Statistical Year Book, 1991.

The above policies have been launched with the conviction that they will lead to rapid rates of industrial growth and exports, through first, high inflows of foreign investment and technology; second, higher investment by the domestic private sector; third, increased efficiency in both the public and private sectors; and fourth, increased competitiveness in domestic and foreign markets both in terms of price and quality.

## Industrial Restructuring in Wake of Structural Adjustment

As we have indicated in earlier sections of this paper, the process of liberalising and opening up the Indian economy was a gradual one which picked up speed in the second half of the 1980s. Under the influence of this process, Indian industry and infrastructure began to undergo a shift and a restructuring in the 1980s relative to the character they had acquired by the late 1970s. The structural adjustment policies introduced in 1991 are likely to intensify and accelerate the trends set in motion in the 1980s. Of the various elements that make up the new industrial policy package of the Indian government, the following can be expected to have the greatest impact:

(a) Abolition of the licensing system, in conjunction with the abolition of the restrictions on growth in investment size, production capacity and product lines of individual enterprises.

(b) Automatic approval of majority equity holdings by foreign capital, and of foreign technology collaboration agreements, in the 34 high priority areas.

(c) Unrestricted imports of capital goods, technical knowledge and managerial expertise, in a large number of industrial and infrastructure! branches, on the condition that these are paid for in convertible hard foreign exchange brought in through foreign investment by the enterprise in question.

(d) Allowing up to one-quarter of the investment capital of a small firm to be owned by other firms.

(e) Enforcing penalties on the public sector for non-performance.

We now examine the differential impact that the new policies are likely to have on the restructuring process that had been set in motion before 1991.

**Oligopoly**

From the mid-80s onwards, the consumer goods sector, both non-durables and durables, has shown much more dynamism than the intermediate and capital goods sectors. At present it also leads the other two in terms of the share of total industrial output and profits. This performance is traceable to themacro-economic policy shift of the Indian state in the mid-80s to stimulate consumer demand by the urban and rural middle income groups. With restrictions on investment size, production capacity and product lines gone, the fight between the big industrial-cum-trading houses will greatly intensify to grab as much of the consumer goods cake as possible. The scene is set for the further spreading of the cancer of oligopoly that has affected the Indian body industrial and economic so long, with its ills of market rigging, price fixing, indifference to quality and predilection for kickbacks.

The impressive growth of the small-scale sector over the last four decades has taken place under the protection offered by two policies: first, the reservation of certain commodities for the small scale sector from which the large firms were excluded; second, severe restrictions on how much of a small firm's capital can be owned by other firms. While 'commodity reservation' is still in place in the new industrial policy, the capital ownership restriction has been substantially weakened. One can foresee how through the '25 per cent rule' mentioned above, large companies will increase the scope and magnitude of their control, de facto if not de jure, of the more dynamic and profitable small firms, something that has been conducted so far on a modest scale by undercover proxy ownership. This in turn will indirectly further erode the protection offered by commodity reservation. The small firms that come under the grip of large ones will perforce follow the economic rationale of the latter in replacing labour-intensive technology by labour-displacing ones, and local resources by non-local ones.

These moves will further entrench and accelerate the decades old process of concentration of the more profitable goods in the hands of a limited number of large firms, with the small scale sector left to produce for the poor majority. The brunt of this scale-encroachment will be borne mainly by the following historically most dynamic branches of the small scale sector, which today account for between 40 and 90 per cent of the branch wise value added (see Table 4.2 in Sandesara 1992): food processing, beverages, tobacco, textiles, wood and leather products, and simpler metal products and parts, including household utensils.

**Production for Domestic Marker Vs. Foreign Market**

Among the 34 so-called 'high priority' areas that the Indian government has opened up for majority equity ownership by foreign capital, there is not a single consumer goods branch. This is not a coincidence. It is entirely consistent with the post-independence industrialisation strategy of the Indian state to safeguard the consumer goods sector for domestic private capital. On the other hand, the success of the new industrial and economic policy package is entirely predicated on being able to attract hard currency investment and high tech from the OECD and east Asian regions, to improve the competitiveness of Indian industrial goods, in particular of consumer durables, on the world market. It is hoped that foreign investors will be prepared to accept a non-controlling role in Indian firms in return for attractive profits in export markets. However, it is no secret that the OECD and east Asian investors are primarily interested in getting into the growing middle and upper income markets within India. They are less motivated about helping Indian firms improve their export competitiveness. The interplay of these diverse interests is likely to lead to a major restructuring of the large scale sector in Indian industry along the following lines. It applies to both the private and public sectors, in all the three use-based sectors (those illustrative examples mentioned below which belong to the intermediate and capital goods sectors are taken from the Indian government's priority list):

(1) Firms which are mainly geared to the domestic market, with no foreign investment.. but using imported earlier standard-tech designs.

*Examples:* Textiles, beverages, radios, television sets, refrigerators, watches, pharmaceuticals, chemicals, fertilisers, paper and pulp, rubber, cement, building materials, machine tools, industrial and agricultural machinery, passenger and commercial vehicles, railway equipment.

(2) Firms with foreign investment and imported high tech producing largely for the domestic market, but also attempting to export a part of their output.

*Examples:* Colour television, videos, compact discs, washing machines, household gadgets, passenger vehicles, cuticles, chemicals, pre-fabricated building materials; electrical, electronic and telecommunication equipment.

(3) Primarily export-oriented companies with foreign investment and imported high tech.

*Examples:* A range of the latest microprocessor based consumer durables and household gadgets, chemicals, computers, computerised equipment in electricals and electronics, Pharma ceuticals, chemicals, pre-fabricated building materials, electrical, electronic and telecommunication equipment.

**Table 4: Educational Levels in 1975 and 1985: Numbers Enrolled as Percentage of Age Group**

| *Country* | *Secondary Education* | | *Higher Education* | |
|---|---|---|---|---|
| | *1* | *2* | *3* | *4* |
| India | 1975 | 1985 | 1975 | 1985 |
| South Korea | 28 56 | 38 90 | 8.6 10.3 | 6.4 34.2 |

*Source:* UNESCO, -Statistical Yearbook, 1991.

**Table 5: Enrolment in Higher Education in Natural Science, Mathematics, Engineering and Computer Science**

| *Country* | *Year* | *No. in Thousands* | *As %age of Total Enrolment in Higher Education* |
|---|---|---|---|
| India | 1985 | 1234 | 27.6 |
| South Korea | 1989 | 384 | 24.3 |

*Source:* UNESCO, Statistical Yearbook, 1991.

**Retrenching of Public of Public Sector**

Until the mid-1980s, the public sector had been assured a privileged and pampered place in the industrial and technological advance of India. That era is coming to a close. The new policy directive is to hold public sector firms firmly accountable for their future non-performance, entailing the real possibility of cutbacks and closures. In addition, there is the stated policy intention of privatising 20 per cent of the government holdings in the public sector firms. In the none too distant future this may mean that the public sector will have to vacate its place in a range of industries and technologies. Into which of these gaps the private sector, both domestic and foreign, will step depends on their perceived profitability. Clearly, many will not be. This heralds a radical reordering of the industrial scene in India, the contours of which are not yet discernible. The old self-imposed imperative of wanting to make nearly everything from mirrors to missiles has lost its relevance.

**Technological Implications of Structural Adjustment**

In the first section of this paper we reviewed the main features of the technological scene in India on the eve of structural adjustment. We noticed there that the characteristics attained during the 'closed economy and strong state intervention era' had begun to alter under the pressure of liberalising and opening up of the economy in the 1980s. Chief among the features in the late 1980s were lack of dynamism in technology absorption, absence of technological innovation and design capacity, spread of technological dualism, lack of significant structural change in the skill composition of the workforce, poor educational base, etc. We argue below that the new policy regime introduced by SAP is likely to entrench these negative features rather than help to overcome them. The increasing dualism and polarisation in the area of technology and skills is one of the outcomes of the conflict between rival interests: domestic capital vs foreign capital, the Indian state vs the Bretton Woods institutions, production for the domestic market vs the export market, the public sector vs the private sector, the 'sick' public sector vs the 'healthy' public sector, the large scale vs the small scale, etc. One among several major consequences of these processes will be that medium and large scale firms will speed up their retooling with imported high tech, abandoning domestically produced standard-tech as fast as they can afford. In contrast, the small-scale sector will continue to depend on locally produced technology, becoming by stages its principal customer.

### Acquisition of New Skills

As indicated earlier in our analytical framework, high tech is characterised by high values in the degree of automation, science-relatedness and research-intensity. The high values of these three features are now built into most industrial and infrastructural branches of the OECD countries, and present OECD research is geared to making them ever higher. Any contemporary technology from the OECD that India acquires with foreign equity will be of this kind, irrespective of whether the product or the process is 'classical' or not, e.g., metallurgy, industrial machinery, vehicles, cement, wood, glass, rubber, paper, printing, food processing, beverages, seeds, etc (see the Indian government's list of 'the privileged 34' in the Appendix). One immediate consequence will be that Indian firms will have to retrain their engineers and technicians to use, maintain and repair the new technology. Various branches of high tech share a common base in certain new generic fields of knowledge in science and engineering. There is therefore good grounds for thinking that a substantial part of the retraining should be common to most firms, while the more narrowly specialised activity-specific skills could be imparted inside the firm. Since top quality and hands-on practicality are of the essence in such retraining, there are but a few institutions in India who can be entrusted with this task.

A number of questions have to be addressed urgently: who should mount common retraining courses, how should the costs be shared, where should the courses be located, is there any credible national expertise available to impart the training or is one obliged to rely heavily on expatriate expertise, etc. The private and the public sector should jointly create an independent-minded task force, with no vested interests, to consider the questions and draft a strategy for retraining on a national basis.

Usually, the introduction of high tech renders most semi-skilled, and some skilled work, redundant. (The limited number of skilled workers who will be retained by firms in the transition to high tech will have to undergo retraining of the kind offered to technicians.) Since, under the present relatively just Indian labour laws, workers cannot in effect be retrenched, the private and the public sector will have to find other areas of work for them. This will be a huge challenge and a growing one. There are as yet no signs that any constructive, humane and productive strategy has been crafted to deal with this challenge. It would be a tremendous waste of the existing technological capacity of India if the technical capabilities of 'potentially redundant' workers are not used productively. Theoretically, there are three ways in which their capacities can be so used.

First, if one has confidence in the official prognosis that SAP will usher in an era of very high growth rates, the new industrial enterprises, both large and small, may be expected to absorb some of the retrenched workforce. But one cannot be sanguine about it. The 1980s relatively high annual rates of industrial growth of 8 per cent occurred with almost no growth in jobs in the registered organised industrial sector. Growth in output was achieved through higher-labour and technological productivities. The high tech transition will in all likelihood attempt to continue this trend of high output growth with low job growth; that is in fact what it will have to do, if all that is asked of it in terms of high productivity, efficiency, quality and market competitiveness has to be delivered. So this route is likely to remain closed for the redundant workforce.

From the recent computations of Ghose (1993) one can infer that labour productivity in manufacturing during the second half of the 1980s maintained the increased positive levels it had attained in the first half. This trend seems less due to increasing skill content of the workforce than to increasing capital intensity of the means of production, retrenchment of labour and the phenomenon of jobless growth. Further, as we have argued elsewhere [Bhagavan 1992], productivity is not merely a function of shop floor efficiency, but also of crucial externalities such as transport and energy infrastructure. It is not a coincidence that the boost in investment in railways, electric power generation and fossil fuel production preceded the 1980s increases in both industrial output and productivity.

The second route is through small scale industry. It is traditionally more labour-intensive than large industry. It would be ideally suited to the levels of skill that the workers have. But to absorb labour at the rate required, it will have to grow at a much greater pace than it is now doing. The wind is apparently blowing in the opposite direction. Potential small scale investors are fighting shy of getting in, saying that the competition is fierce and market demand is stagnant.

The third route is a return to Keynes, with massive public investment in modern energy, transport and communication infrastructure, public civil engineering projects and social services. This will create massive numbers of new jobs, while at the same time conserving, upgrading and increasing the technological capabilities of the workforce.

In the present age of SAP-hegemony the third route may sound like science fiction, given the fierce hostility of the begetters of SAP—the IMF and the World Bank—to anything that smells remotely Keynesian. But they may be forced to temper their market fundamentalism under the pressure of the new employment-creating forces gathering pace in western Europe. At the European Union (EU) summit meeting held in Corfu, Greece, in June 1994, the heads of the EU governments endorsed the neo-Keynesian proposals contained in the white paper of Jacques Delors, President of the European Commission, 'to create massive numbers of new jobs based on new skills. This is to be accomplished mainly through the Trans-European Networks (TENS) Programme comprising 11 transport and communication projects. To quote from the *Guardian* (June 1994), "the summit agreed to step up governments' role in stimulating 'the unprecedented technological revolution' which can lead to developments in tele working, distance learning, road and air traffic management, health care networks and electronic tendering". The Delors proposals are the product of the new economic thinking that has emerged in western Europe over the last few years to grapple with the task of recovering from the disaster of the Reagan-Thatcher era of new liberalism' [Lane 1993; Keegan 1993; Lipietz 1993].

Since technological dualism will continue to deepen in India, the question arises as to how to cater to the technological upgrading of the small scale sector, which as we have seen above, will be even more crucial in the SAP-era than it was before SAP. The market, as one knows too well by now, will not do it unassisted. In fact, the small scale sector in India owes its existence and growth to state protection. Because of its tremendous heterogeneity and extremely wide geographical dispersal, national technology suppliers cannot individually effectively inform and service this sector.

This prompts the suggestion that the state actively promotes the idea of small industrialists' associations themselves establishing technology estates in all medium-sized towns to provide technological information to the local small investors in the local language. The information should be backed up by regular demonstrations of nationally produced hardware and software. As these estates find their feet, they will also take on the role of channels of communication between the users and the domestic producers of technology, which, it is to be hoped, will bring about user-driven improvements, incremental or otherwise.

**Technology Absorption**

About 1,200 industrial firms in India have in-house R and D units. The most qualified work they do is technology absorption; technology design and innovation are at present beyond their capabilities and resources. In the transition to imported high tech, these R and D units are already confronting, and will continue to confront, the challenge of re-skilling themselves to absorb the new technology. The kind of re-skilling called for often involves a shift in their technological paradigm. It will demand of them that they not only theoretically understand the new concepts and the new way of reasoning, but also translate that understanding into shop-floor practice.

The present in-house R and D units, which have evolved slowly to deal with the pre-high tech situation, cannot be 're-jigged' overnight to take on the new challenge. There is little doubt that their capacity to absorb technology will go through a longish period of serious decline. Older professionals who are the intellectual leaders in their R and D units are likely to find that they cannot make the transition. A vicious circle of stress conditions leading to poor performance will set in.

Although the decline cannot be arrested in the short term, certain measures need to be put in place fairly soon to create the R and D capacity in the medium term that firms will need, if high tech is not to remain forever a 'black box with buttons attached' for Indian industry. To this end, the private and public sectors should together commission experts (preferably from high tech exporting countries) to analyse the entire complex of problems and suggest strategies for overcoming them. Mere increases in hardware and software resources, in salaries and perks, and in intra-firm status, will not by themselves be sufficient to generate the motivation and the ambition to solve problems, which only intellectual passion can. Therefore one of the keys will be finding fresh, new recruits with the right cast of mind from the alumni of India's few high quality science and engineering faculties to join the R and D teams. That will not be an easy task given the preference of the brightest professionals to emigrate to North America or Singapore.

**Education and Manpower**

The likely impact of structural adjustment on the public funding of education in developing countries in general is best summarised in the following words from a World Bank study [Noss 1992]:

Adjustment measures (undertaken with or without World Bank assistance) affect education through changes at the macro and micro levels of the economy. Adjustment at the macro level often implies a combination of budget containment measures for the public education system, limited access to post primary public education and higher user fees for education services at the secondary and tertiary levels. At the micro level, changes in household incomes and prices (user fees, reduced student subsidies) directly influence the demand for education by altering the opportunity cost of attending school. Household incomes also affect health and nutrition status, and thus indirectly influence attendance and learning. Finally, adjustment affects education through changes in markets and infrastructure (resulting from currency devaluation, fiscal and monetary restraint, and price liberalisation) that affect supply of education services and the opportunity cost of attending school.

In plain English what the above-mentioned measures could mean for secondary and higher education in India is first, cuts in public funding, accompanied by the charging of fees; second, a decrease in the number of pupils and students from poorer households; third, a further deterioration of the public education system; and fourth, the strengthening of private education to the benefit of the higher income households.

To go down the route charted by SAP in the area of education is to jump from the frying pan into the fire. India's development ideology notwithstanding, the Indian government has over the last 40 years neglected primary and secondary education in comparison with higher (tertiary) education. Since the education system has been, and continues to be, almost entirely in the hands of the Indian state, it cannot disclaim responsibility for the inequities and the utter lack of quality that have developed at all levels in the system [Shatrugna 1993; Upendranath 1993b].

The industrial and technological progress of India needs precisely the opposite of what the SAP recommends in education. A rapid advance on a broad front is only possible if the educational and technical levels of all the young in India is raised as a matter of the greatest urgency. That is impossible in the Indian context without increased massive support from the state, but a support that is administered in a radically different way than at present. The need of the hour is not SAP-inspired dismantling of the public education system, but a revolutionary transformation of it to raise the quantity and quality of really skilled young people. What the present system is imparting is not education, but bits of ritual paper certifying that this or that exam has been passed with this or that grade.

To take a leaf out of India's neighbours in east Asia, their spectacular success in both economic and social development would not have been possible without their single-minded simultaneous pursuit of universalisation of and high quality in primary and secondary education. In quality tests in science and mathematics administered in the early 1990s to high school pupils across a representative sample of the OECD and the developing countries, with India included, South Korea topped the list, with Japan coming next, western Europe and North America on their heels, and India so far behind as to be invisible in the race.

That said, there is most definitely a need for draconian measures to convert the present. Higher education system from its present degraded state of being one vast conveyor belt graduate factory into a system that actually imparts knowledge. A re-structuring of public funding based on the criteria of social equity, quality and merit, while simultaneously encouraging higher income groups to take advantage of privatised institutions, would be the strategy to follow.

The present system of government national laboratories and institutes has outlived its original rationale. It is demonstrably not contributing to significant innovation in science and technology. It impact on industry has been minimal. The move by the present Indian government to progressively reduce its commitment to this moribund system is a wise one. However, that does not mean that the state can afford not to fund scientific and technological R and D—quite the contrary. Again, as with the educational system as a whole, the state needs to pump vastly more resources into R and D, but along the lines of an entirely new strategy. What the new national R and D system should look like and how it should be put together are issues should be publicly debated in India. The ideas that have recently emerged in the advanced industrialised countries on "national innovation systems" would be of seminal value in such a debate and in arriving at future policy decisions [Nelson 1993].

# 2

# *Technological Capability in Indian Electronics Industry Under Economic Liberalisation*

## Introduction

During the period of economic liberalisation the number of foreign collaborations in electronics has been increasing at a much faster rate than in the industrial sector as a while [Joseph and Narayana 1993]. This acceleration in the rate of foreign collaborations is likely to increase the technological dependence of Indian electronics industry unless the import of technology is backed by in-house R and D effort for its absorption, adaptation and innovation.

The technological capability of an enterprise is argued to be a function of indigenous research and development, technology imports and relation between the two [Blumenthal 1979]. The import of technologies may either substitute or complement (or a combination of both) indigenous R and D. The available empirical evidence on the nature of relationship between the two has been rather mixed in the case of Indian industries. Katrak (1989) found that the imports of technology helped to promote in-house R and D, but the stimulative impact of the former on the latter was 'limited' especially for the complex technologies. The nature of influence of two alternative modes of technology imports, namely, foreign direct investment (FDI) and licensing agreements, on in-house R and D spending was examined by Kumar (1987). His results indicated that the relationship was of substitution in the case of FDI mode of technology import but it was expected to be dominated by complementarily in the other case. For a sample of 100 Indian engineering firms for the year 1978, Lall (1983) found the royalty payments to be positively related to R and D expenditure (both variables being taken as a percentage of sales) and therefore confirmed the existence of complementary relationship. In another study, using Reserve Bank of India Survey data for 10 years (i e, from 1964-65 to 1969-70 and again from 1977-78 to 1980-.81), Subrahmanian (1987) showed the existence of a very strong complementary relationship except in the case of foreign subsidiaries and concluded that the Indian firms generally moved along a "technology dependence-independence continuum", primarily because of the greater emphasis laid on the in-house R and D.

Another set of studies by Subrahmanian (1991), Siddharthan (1988) and Mani (1993) treated electronics as a separate sector. Subrahmanian found that the technology-importers did not undertake significantly higher R and D expenditure than the technology non-importers. Siddharthan made a distinction between the public sector and the private sector units, and showed the existence of complementary relationship between import of technology and in-house R and D effort (both taken as percentage of sales) for the private sector firms whereas for the public sector firms evidence indicated to a substitution relationship. However, the existence of complementary relationship in the public sector was confirmed by Mani but he showed that the degree of complementarity was weakest in the electronics sector which had witnessed fast changing technological advances.

These studies analysed the nature of the relationship between the expenditure on imported technology and R and D on the basis of the industry-level data but here this relationship will be examined by using enterprise-level time-series data for some of the public sector units (PSUs) operating in the field of electronics. The fact that an enterprise's imports of technology may affect its R and D can be studied by an empirical analysis of two questions relevant to the R and D behaviour of enterprises in the electronics sector. The first question is whether the level of R and D expenditure is higher amongst the technology importers than in the non-importers. This question also considers whether the expenditures on R and D are likely to differ between certain types of enterprises: large and small, private and public, indigenous and foreign-owned. The second question is whether the technological capabilities of some of the PSUs both at the central as well as at the state levels have been increasing as a result of their R and D expenditure over time.

This article is organised in the following manner. Section II discusses the procedures for the empirical tests. Section III deals with the sources of data and methods of measurement of variables. Section IV reports the results. Section V summarises the main findings.

**Procedures for Empirical Analysis**

The first question will be examined by introducing a dummy variable in a regression equation. The regression equation will also consider the influence of enterprise size (measured by the annual sales turnover and denoted by 'S') to find out whether larger enterprises undertake proportionately more R and D (denoted by 'RD' in regression equations) than the smaller ones. It will also be interesting to study whether the R and D expenditure is higher for that enterprise which has greater experience in adapting imported technologies. It is, therefore, proposed to include the age of the R and D unit as a proxy for the experience of an enterprise in R and D activities. The regression test will take the form

$$\log RD = a+b \log S+c \log A+d\, TM \quad (1)$$ where,

TM = 1 for technology importers

= 0 for non-importers of technology

and A = age of the R and D unit measured from the date of establishment.

The log-linear regression form will be used because it will readily show the elasticity of R and D with respect to size (S). Thus, if the estimated coefficient of S turns out to be less than unity, it will mean that an increase in enterprise size leads to a less than proportionate increase in R and D. Alternatively, one can also examine whether the R and D intensity (RD/S) increases with the size of the enterprise and age of the R and D unit and whether it is significantly higher amongst the technology importers than the non-importers by fitting a regression equation of the following form,

log RD/S = a, + b, log S + c, log A + d, TM (2)

If the estimated value for b in equation (1) turns out to be less than unity then this will imply a negative value for the estimated B1 in the equation (2). One can also measure the influence of technology by a slope dummy defined as TM, = TM* log S in place of the intercept dummy TM in the equations (1) and (2).

The R and D behaviour may differ depending on the type of the enterprises such as, private and public, indigenous and foreign-owned, etc. Since the R and D projects of PSUs are financially supported by the department of electronics (DOE)' we will run a regression equation of the type

log RD/S = a2 + b, log S + e PUB (3)

where, PUB= 1 for the public sector units

= 0, otherwise

to find out whether the R and D intensity is significantly higher in the PSUs than the private-sector units.

The imperfections in the international technology market may have different impact upon: (a) indigenous enterprises and (b) subsidiaries of foreign enterprises. The RBI survey (1974) found that companies which had foreign financial collaboration were comparatively less active in setting up R and D units. It has also been observed that the foreign collaborated companies demonstrate a longer lag in adaptation and assimilation of the imported technology [Pillai 1979]. Among different forms of technology transfer the degree of control exercised by the transferor was found to be maximum in the case of the foreign direct investment [Balasubrahmanian 1973]. So a subsidiary of a foreign multinational may face greater restrictions on the extent to which an imported technology can be adapted. It will, therefore, be interesting to find out whether the research intensities of the foreign-controlled enterprises (i e, those with 25 per cent or more foreign equity following RBI definition) are significantly less than those of the indigenous enterprises by running a regression equation of the following type

log RD/S = a3 + b, log S + FDI (4)

where, FDI = 1 for foreign-controlled enterprises
= 0 for indigenous enterprises

Let us now consider the second question which is concerned with the inter-temporal changes in the technological capabilities of some of the PSUs. The expenditure on technology import (direct cost of foreign collaborations) of an enterprise represents the degree of technological dependence whereas its expenditure on R and D efforts reflects its internal technological capacity. The technological capability of an enterprise is said to be increasing so long as the proportionate increase in the R and D spending exceeds that of expenditure on imported technologies. The logic is that as a firm spends more on R and D, its knowledge on technology becomes richer. Since the cost of technology transfer depends largely upon the relative bargaining strength of the buyer and the seller, with a better technological knowledge the buyer can now be at a better position in bargaining and thereby, can bring down the cost of technology imports [Teece 1977; Lall 1980]. Following the lines suggested by Katrak (1985) we adopt a procedure for measuring the technological capability. Let 'EM' denote the expenditures on imported technologies. The 'average propensity to adapt' is RD/ EM. An increase in this propensity will imply an improvement in an enterprise's technological capability. Since it is a static concept we also introduce the marginal propensity to adapt as 9RD/9EM. Now the ratio between the marginal and average propensity to adapt (9RD/9EM/RD/EM) will be the "elasticity of R and D with respect to the technology import". This elasticity is a measure of the relative change in R and D to a proportionate change in the cost of technology import. The data of RD and EM will be used to fit a regression equation of the following form to estimate the elasticity

log RD = a + Plog EM (5) Here the regression coefficient P will give an estimate of the elasticity. A value of P greater than unity will be interpreted as evidence of increasing technological capability of the enterprise. Conversely, if the estimated p is less than unity the result.

**Data and Measurement of Variables**

Empirical analysis in the framework suggested above requires two sets of data. One set of data was collected from Compendium on In-House R and D Centres, 1990 published by the department of scientific and industrial research (DSIR) on the basis of a survey of the firms registered with it. This compendium provides quantitative data such as, R and D expenditure, sales turnover, the year of establishment of the R and D unit and also qualitative information on the basis of which it is possible to separate out technology-importers and non-importers, public sector and private sector units, foreign-controlled enterprises and indigenous enterprises.

The second set of data on the R and D expenditure, sales turnover, expenditure on imported technology were collected from the annual reports of the ECIL, SCL and GCEL. All these variables were measured at the constant prices with reference to the base year 1981-82. The items belonging to the capital account of R and D expenditure were deflated by the price index of machinery and machine tools including electrical machinery and the revenue account expenditure of R and D of a unit was deflated by the consumer price index for urban non-manual employees of that place where the unit is situated.' These price indices were obtained from H.L. Chandhok's (1990) 'India Data Base'. Since this source provides price-index data up to 1988-89, the price-index for the year 1989-90 was collected from the Report of Currency and Finance published by RBI. With regard to the sales turnover the sales items of each unit were identified and their prices were obtained from the Guide to Electronics Industry, a DOE publication. In the case of the units selling more than one item, a weighted price index was constructed where the share of each item in the total sales turnover was taken as the weight. The direct cost of technology import (EM) was measured as the outflow of foreign exchange due to the technical know-how fees, royalty and interest payment, professional consultancy fees, advances to foreign suppliers of technology and the imports of capital goods as the imported capital equipment may embody a certain

**Table 1: Major Products and Foreign Technology Collaboration Agreements of Three Public Sector Units in Electronics**

| *Name of the Unit (Year Incorporated)* | *Major Products* | *Foreign Technology Collaboration Agreements* | |
|---|---|---|---|
| | | *Technology Supplier* | *Products* |
| Electronics | Digital computer systems | Siemens, West Germany (erstwhile) | SPC telex exchange |
| Corporation of India | Colour television receiver sets | Norsk Data, Norway | Remote telemetry units |
| (ECIL) (1967) | Black and White TVs Telex | Ferranti, UK NEC, Japan | Deigital transreceivers Line |
| (Central Public Unit) | exchange equipment Nuclear power plant instrumentation | Kabelmetal Electro, West Germany (erstwhile) | if Sight Antennas |
| | Control panel, Defence | Control Data Indo-Asia Co, | Mainframe computers |
| | equipment Two-way wireless | (CDC), USA FAG, | Microprocessor-based |
| | communication sets | West Germany (former) | thickness gauges |
| | Passive components | Harris Ferinon, Canada | Communication system |
| | Printed circuit boards | Thermocoax Et Cie, France | Self-powered neutron detector |
| | High power amplifier systems | RACAL, UK | V-UHF receivers |
| | Antennae with feed (of various sizes) | Varian, USA | 400W HPA |
| Semiconductor Complex (SCL) | Bipolar/MOS large scale integrated circuits | Hitachi, Japan | Digital electronic watch models |

| | | | |
|---|---|---|---|
| (1978) (Central public sector unit) | LSI/VLSI devices Bipolar/ MOS large | Americen Microsystems (AMI), USA | 5micron and micron CMDS and MOS silicon gate technologies |
| | Integrated chips (LSI/VLSI) chips (silicon chips) | Citizen Watch Co, Japan Rockwell International, USA | Assembly of ECB |
| | Electronic circuit blocks Printed circuit boards | CIT Alcatel, France | Microprocessor and peripheral devices LSI devices |
| Gujarat Communication and Electronics (GCEL), (1975) (State public sector unit) | Radio relay communication equipment Instrument landing system Video Tape Recorder | Genelcom, a subsidiary of GEC, Canada Sony Corporation, Japan Robert Bosch, West Germany (erstwhile) Siemens, West Germany (erstwhile) Rohde and Schwarz, West Germany (erstwhile) Ampex (country not available) | Extended range VHF equipment U-MATIC Video equipment and high band VCRs Video tape recorder Electronic telephone instruments FM transmitters Digital video effects. |

kind of know-how. The price indices for these items are not available. During the period of our study, the rupee experienced a continuous depreciation against the major currencies of the world and our domestic rate of inflation was much higher than in other developed countries from which the technologies were imported. So, the time-series figures of the direct costs of technology imports were deflated by the real effective exchange rate (REER) which is a weighted average of bilateral price-deflated nominal exchange rates.4 A problem in searching for an empirical relationship between the import of technology and R and D is that latter activity may be undertaken a year (or more) after the former. Considering this possibility our data werg further analysed and it was decided to regress the R and D expenditure of any year upon the average of the technology expenditure of that year and a year before.

**Empirical Results**

The first question was examined by running few regression equations [discussed in Section II] and the results are reported in Table 2.

The positive signs of the technology-import dummies TM and TM, in equations (1) to (4) indicate that both the level of R and D expenditure and the R and D intensity were higher amongst the technology importers than the non-importers. Thus, in this sense, it seems that the imports of technology encouraged R and D as the imported technology was required to be adapted to the local conditions. Such a kind of adaptive R and D might also be undertaken in solution of problems such as breakdown of machinery, shortage of imported components, etc. However, this stimulating effect of imported technology upon R and D was limited, since the technology import dummies, at best, could reach only the 5 per cent level of significance.

In equations (1) and (3) the coefficients of log S are positive and significant at the 1 per cent level but less than unity.[5] This indicates that the larger enterprises undertook proportionately less R and D than the smaller ones. This outcome also followed from the fact that the coefficient of log S are negative

**Table 2: Log-Linear Regression Equations Explaining R and D in Electronics Sector**

| *Equations Dependent Variable* | *Constant* | *S* | *A* | *TM* | *TM, PUB* | *FDI* |
|---|---|---|---|---|---|---|
| (1) RD | -.038015 | .31547*** | .05539 | .55065* | | |
| | (-.07347) | (3.7356) | (.37415) | (1.8835) | | |
| (2) RD/S | -.038015 | -.68453*** | .05539 | .55065* | | |
| | (-.07347) | (-8.1059) | (.37415) | (1.8835) | | |
| (3) RD | .13303 | .29723*** | | | .07858** | |
| | (.27873) | (3.4635) | | | (2.0731) | |
| (4) RD/S | .13303 | -.70277*** | | | .07858** | |
| | (.27873) | (-8.1889) | | | (2.0731) | |
| (5) RD/S | -.039892 | -.60782*** | | | -.27558 | |
| | (-.08191) | (-7.6677) | | | (-.74692) | |
| (6) RD/S | -.029403 | -.61308*** | | | | -.14961 |
| | (-.06020) | (-7.7246) | | | | (-.40500) |

| *Equations* | *Dependent Variables* | *R2* | *R2* | *F* |
|---|---|---|---|---|
| (1) | RD | .33650 | .30096 | 9.4670 |
| (2) | RD/S | .55107 | .52702 | 22.9137 |
| (3) | RD | .34336 | .32022 | 14.8962 |
| (4) | RD/S | .55564 | .54005 | 35.6378 |
| (5) | RD/S | .52677 | .51017 | 31.7247 |
| (6) | RD/S | .52351 | .50679 | 31.3126 |

*Notes:* The regressions are based on the data of 60 enterprises that undertake R and D of which 34 were importers of technology, t -values are shown in parentheses

*** indicates significance at 1 per cent level (two-tailed test)

** indicates significance at 5 per cent level (two-tailed test)

* indicates significance at 10 percent level (two-tailed test)

Source: See Section HI.

in the equations (2), (4), (5) and (6) indicating significantly lower research-intensities in the larger enterprises. It seemed that the greater market power and the absence of competitive pressures reduced larger enterprises' incentive for R and D.

In equations (1) and (2) the coefficients of log A are positive but not statistically significant. Thus, the experience of an enterprise in R and D activities did not make any significant influence upon its R and D expenditure or its R and D intensity.

The two dummy variables were introduced in equations (5) and (6) to examine the R and D behaviour of certain types of enterprises: public and private and indigenous and foreign-owned. It can be observed from equation (5) that the research intensities did not differ significantly between the public and the private sector enterprises. One would have expected higher research-intensities for the PSUs since their R and D projects are generally financed by DOE. But, it seems that in an era of liberalisation, both the public and the private sector units prefer to import package technology which does not require much R and D activities. The equation (6) shows that the research intensities of the foreign-controlled enterprises were not significantly less than those of the indigenous enterprises. A possible explanation is that the dummy is reflecting two opposing effects: thus whereas indigenous enterprises might have greater scope for determining their own R and D efforts, they might also have relatively less assistance from their foreign suppliers in the assimilation of the imported technology.

The second question is concerned with the technological capabilities of some of the PSUs in the field of electronics. This question was examined by pooling the time-series data pertaining to the two CPSUs (i.e., EC1L and SCL) and one SPSU (i.e., GCEL) and a regression analysis was undertaken to obtain the following regression equation

log RD = -.074656 +1.1044 log EM

(-.15059) (3.4289)

+ 1.9906 D, + .21940 D2

(3.6882) (.33309)

-.99699 D, log EM -.41715 D2 log EM

(-2.9613) (-1.1663)

$R^2$ = .77880 $R^2$ = .72614

Figures in brackets denote t-values.

**Table 3: Elasticity Coefficients of Three Public Sector Units**

| *Name of unit* | *Elasticity Coefficients* | | *t-values* |
|---|---|---|---|
| (i) GCEL | $\beta_1$ | =1.1044*** | 3.4289 |
| (ii) ECIL | $\beta_1 + \beta_4$ | =.10741 | 1.0954 |
| (iii) SCL | $\beta_1 + \beta_5$ | = .68725*** | 4.4189 |

*Note:**** denotes significance at 1 per cent level.

*Source:* Computed from the annual reports of ECIL, SCL and GCEL.

The elasticity coefficients of the three PSUs are

represented in Table 3.

The regression results establish the existence of complementary relationship between R and D and technology-import expenditure for all the three PSUs, although the relationship was not statistically significant in the case of ECIL (Table 3). The elasticity coefficient exceeded unity only in the case of GCEL. So, folio wing our definition, among the three PSUs only GCEL was able to strengthen its technological capability through its R and D efforts. Although being a state public sector unit the scale of operation of GCEL, measured in terms of average sales turnover, was much lower than the two CPSUs but its research-intensity was the highest (Table 4). GCEL also enjoyed an increase in the propensity to adapt over time, whereas it declined in the case of ECIL (Table 5). However, the propensity to adapt increased only marginally for SCL.

It can be observed from the Table 4 that GCEL was a profit-earning enterprise so apart from the financial help from DOE. It was able to generate surplus funds which could be used to back up the import of technology with indigenous R and D. It can be recalled here that the telecommunication sector was reserved for the PSUs only till mid-1980s. Thus, GCEL, under the influence of government's protective policy was able to facilitate its technological capability. On the other hand, ECIL was also a profit-earning enterprise but its growth rate of R and D expenditure was so low that it could not match with the very high growth rate of its expenditure on imported technology as a result not only its propensity to adapt declined, it also experienced an increase in the import intensity of the technology over time (Table 5). With the shift in the government's policy from 'protectionism' to 'liberalisation', ECIL which had not entered into any foreign collaboration till 1978, signed five foreign collaboration agreements in 1986 alone. It also ranked seventh among the 10 largest importers of foreign technology in the Indian public sector having a total of 15 such collaboration approvals till 1986. ECIL was engaged in manufacturing indigenous computers during 1970s but it started assembling CKD/SKD kits imported from its foreign collaborators during 1980s. This kind of 'kit-culture' provided very little scope for undertaking any worthwhile R and D activities. The large number of foreign collaboration agreements of ECIL accounted for a very high rate of increase in its expenditures on the imported technologies which were not backed up with indigenous R and D efforts in the same intensity as a result the technological dependence of ECIL increased over time (Table 5). Moreover, the technologies imported were not the state-of-the-art. The electronics telex exchange technology from Siemens and mainframe technology from CDC when brought by ECIL were about to be phased out in the global market. It should be noted here, that GCEL did not enter the export markets whereas the two CPSUs were engaged in exporting their products. It is also possible that the CPSUs were less assisted by their foreign suppliers in the assimilation of the imported technologies as they were viewed as potential competitors in the export markets. This kind of 'oligopolistic squeezing' very often hinders the development of technological capabilities of Indian enterprises" [Bagchi 1982; Alam 1985]. It should be noted from Table 5 that the R and D intensities of all the three PSUs declined over time. In this sense, PSUs are becoming less R and D oriented and the efficiency of resource utilisation (measured as the ratio of value-added to total production, [Bagchi 1986] also declined during the period of liberalisation (Table 5).

However, among the three PSUs only GCEL, even being in a state sector, has shown better performance so far as the development of technological capability is concerned. It even developed Time Division Multiple Access (TDMA) Communication system when the concept of TDMA had yet to get transformed into practical hardware and moreover, no field proven equipment of this type was available in the country. This project was, however, supported by DOE by providing GCEL with R and D funds for the design, development and

**Table 4: Sales Turnover, R and D Intensity Ratios of Three Public Sector Units (1981-82 = 100 Unless Otherwise Stated)**

| *Name of the Unit* | *Sales Turnover (Rs in Lakh)* | *Profitability (at Current Prices)* | *R and D Intensity* | *Import Intensity of the Technology* |
|---|---|---|---|---|
| ECIL | 13,666.56 | 0.04 | 0.01 | 0.02 |
| SCL | 2,298.50 | (-) 0.02 | 0.17 | 1.31 |
| GCEL | 701.89 | 0.08 | 0.27 | 0.33 |

*Notes:*

(i) These are average figures calculated over the study period of each unit.

(ii) Profitability was measured as the ratio of profit after tax to the gross fixed assets.

(iii) Import intensity of the technology was measured as the ratio of the expenditures on imported technologies to the sales turnover.

(iv) SCL could not achieve break-even operations till 1987-88. Source: Computed from the annual reports of GCEL, SCL and ECIL.

engineering of the system. In barely two years and nine months with a cost of Rs 1.5 crore the TDMA Communication System became a reality. At first, this system was successfully used by Steel Authority of India (SAIL) in its Kiriburu complex and later on, it was also supplied to the Railways, Coal India and the State Electricity. Boards. GCEL, also played a pivotal role in developing Pulse Code Modulation (PCM) Multiplex Equipment which was required for converting our entire communication network into a digital one. Till 1981, to meet requirements prevailing at that time, the department of telecommunication (DOT) had been importing this equipment from Japan. But seeing that there could be large requirements in the Seventh and Eighth Plans, Indian Telephone Industries (ITI), at the instance of the DOT started negotiations with a leading multinational company for acquiring foreign technology to make this equipment. Meanwhile, GCEL offered to Telecommunications Research Centre (TRC) to produce PCM Multiplex Equipment based on TRC's indigenous design and know-how. While doing so GCEL recognised that the per channel Codec design of TRC was superior to the Codec design of the multinational company. Accordingly, GCEL engineered the TRC design, and produced a batch of PCM terminals for field trials by DOT. These trials were satisfactorily completed by the end of 1983. With such excellent progress made by the GCEL-TRC team, the government decided that ITI could not proceed with its proposed technical collaboration with the multinational company for PCM multiplex equipment, but would, instead, also make the equipment as per the GCEL-TRC design [Parthasarathi 1992]. SCL also had its success when it was able to reach 2 micron technology in 1988, without any cost or time overrun starting from 5 micron under its technology up gradation plan.

The government policy of liberalisation encouraged the induction of foreign technologies which were expected to improve our product qualities and to accelerate the growth rate of our exports. This kind of export-led-growth, apart from increasing income and employment, was also likely to ease the foreign exchange burden of our country. It will be interesting to study whether the net earnings of foreign exchange of these PSUs increased during the period of liberalisation. This can be measured with the help of 'Net Foreign Exchange Inflow Ratio' (NFIR) which is defined as

Exports - (Imports of goods + Imports of technologies)

NFIR = Exports

The trends of NFIR for ECIL and SCL are reported in Table 6. The values of NFIR are negative throughout the period under consideration indicating higher outflows of foreign exchange than inflows. The negative trend of NFIR did not show any declining tendency in either case, therefore, it could not be asserted that the import dependence of these CPSUs was decreasing over time. "Thus, the fond hope behind the government's policy of liberalisation has so far shown no sign of materialisation so far as the earnings of foreign exchange are concerned. The import intensity of the electronics industry is very high" and the electronics equipment and components, manufacturing units taken for this study are found to be net spenders of foreign exchange, so one wonders whether a country like India with a weak 'macroeconomic capability'

[Bagchi and Banerjee 1986] can afford to develop new technologies on a massive scale.

## Summary and Conclusions

The liberalisation policy of our government encouraged the import of foreign technologies by Indian enterprises. Here, we have examined whether the technological capabilities of the Indian enterprises in the field of electronics have been increasing as the imports of technologies are expected to stimulate in-house R and D efforts. This was studied first, by introducing dummy variables in a regression analysis which indicated that both the levels of R and D expenditures and the R and D intensity were higher amongst the technology importers than the non-importers. However, the stimulating effect of imported technology upon R and D was found to be limited. Then, the time-series R and D data were regressed upon the data on expenditures on imported technologies of the three public sector units. Although the regression analysis established a complementary relationship between the two variables only one unit was able to increase its technological capability through its R and D efforts. However, all the three units turned out to be net spenders of foreign exchange and their import dependence did not show any definite declining trend over time. The regression also found that the larger enterprises incurred proportionately less R and D expenditures. It was also observed that the R and D intensities did not differ significantly between the public and the private sector enterprises and between the indigenous and the foreign controlled enterprises.

The high growth rate of the electronics industry

during the early 1980s could not be sustained during the late 80s [Joseph and Narayana 1993]. Moreover, the factor productivities also declined over time indicating growing inefficiency in factor use. Here we have observed that the R and D intensities of all the three public sector units declined during the period under study. Although this result cannot be generalised, it cannot be denied either that the Indian enterprises are becoming less R and D oriented due to the emergence of the 'kit-culture'. The government should intervene to ensure that the import is sufficiently backed up with domestic R and D so that apart from increasing the technological capability the efficiency of resource utilisation also increases which is likely to arrest the declining trend in productivity and output.

**Table 6: Trends in NFIR for Two Central Public Sector Units**

| *Year* | *ECIL* | *SCL* |
|---|---|---|
| 1980-81 | (-) 400.87 | |
| 1981-82 | (-) 161.66 | |
| 1982-83 | (-) 74.90 | |
| 1983-84 | (-) 1127.37* | (-) 423.85 |
| 1984-85 | (-) 4.76 | (-) 9503.00 |
| 1985-86 | Not Available | (-) 265.88 |
| 1986-87 | (-) 110.28 | (-) 56.98 |
| 1987-88 | (-) 67.85 | (-) 45.37 |
| 1988-89 | (-) 133.23 | (-) 171. 17 |
| 1989-90 | (-) 110.61 | (-) 1283.50* |

*Notes:* * To calculate NFIR the values of exports were taken to be Rs 1 lakh as the actual export earnings for these two years were nil.

SCL started its commercial production in 1983-84.

*Source:* Computed from the annual reports of ECIL, SCL.

**Table 5: Growth Rates (Compound) of R and D and its Intensity, Expenditure on Imported Technologies and its Intensity, Propensity to Adapt, Sales Turnover and Efficiency of Utilisation of Resources (1981-82=100)**

| *Name of the Unit* | *Sales Turn over* | *Expenditure On Imported Technologies* | *R and D Expen-diture* | *Import Intensity of the Te-chnology* | *Propensity to Adapt* | *R and D Intesity* | *Efficiency of Utilisation of Resources* |
|---|---|---|---|---|---|---|---|
| ECIL | 21.09 | 54.41 | 4.67 | 27.52 | (-) 32.22 | (-) 13.56 | (-) 2.61 |
| SCL | 27.52 | 17.56 | 18.71 | (-) 2.47 | 0.98 | (-) 29.33 | (-) L43 |
| GCEL | 78.96 | 14.27 | 17.80 | H36.15 | 3.09 | (-)34.17 | (-) 3.33 |

## INDIAN SOFTWARE EXPORTS: AN ASSESSMENT

### The Symptoms

The remarkable growth of Indian software exports from a mere Rs. 71 crore in 1987 to Rs. 700 crore in 1993—an increase by a factor of 10 in six years'—has sparked off peculiar syndrome which may have far-reaching consequences in the future. On the one hand, there are high expectations from this sector, and it is firmly believed that this is one of the few areas in which India has the potential to become a global powerhouse. On the other hand, the degree of euphoria, virtually bordering on arrogance, is such that it is apparently believed that nothing much needs to be done in terms of policy support for this sector. This syndrome has been further reinforced by studies which suggest that software exports are likely, in any case, to touch US $ 640 million by 1996, and with a little bit of effort US $ 1 billion is also attainable in the same time frame. As a consequence, the focus has shifted away from the fundamentals to the marginals.

If this sounds like hyperbole, consider the following policy stances. In 1992 the government extended the tax exemption on export profits available to merchandise exporters through Section 80-HHC of the Income Tax Act to software exporters by introducing Section 80-HHE. The difference, however, was that while Section 80-HHC had currency of five years, Section 80-HHE was on an annual basis. As a result, there has been a constant uncertainty regarding the renewal of this section, and hence the expected net profit of the exporter, which has affected all software contracts which span two or more financial years. In such a situation it is almost impossible to fix a firm price for the duration of the contract.

Other than this basic difference between Sections 80-HHC and 80-HHE, the very similarity between the two sections reveals a lack of appreciation by the policy-makers of the characterise tics of the software industry. While framing Section 80-HHC, it was clearly recognised that profits on exports were negligible or even negative for most merchandise, whereas substantial profits were made on domestic sales. Therefore, in order to make this instrument serve as a real export incentive, a method of "profit averaging" was devised so that exporters could actually claim a part of their profit on domestic sales as export profits. This was achieved by multiplying the ratio of export turnover to total turnover and the total profits of the company in calculating 'export profits' for the purposes of this section. Since domestic turnover is usually computed on the ex-factory price, the export turnover was defined as the invoice value less transportation costs in order to maintain consistency.

It can be shown that this formula will overstate

the export profit if two conditions are met: *(a)* the percentage profit margin on domestic sales is higher than on exports; and *(b)* transport costs form a small percentage of export turnover. Both these conditions are met for merchandise, where profit on exports is substantially less than profit on domestic sales and transport costs form only about 3 per cent of the invoice value. Unfortunately, both the formula and the definition of export turnover were retained while formulating Section 80-HHE, thereby substantially reducing the incentive value of this provision and indeed giving rise to a most undesirable characteristic.

The reasons for this contrary effect are first, that in the software sector profits on exports are considerably higher than on domestic sales. As a consequence, profit averaging actually leads to a part of export profits being counted as profit on domestic sales, and thereby being subject to tax. Second, to make matters worse, transport costs for the software sector have been defined to include both international telecommunication charges and the cost of sending employees abroad. These two together can account for as much as 40 per cent of the invoice value in software exports. This causes the share of exports in total turnover to be much less than actual. The net result of this *pari passu,* rather than *mutatis mutandis* application of the provisions of Section 80-HHC to 80-HHE is that not only do the software exporters have to pay tax on legitimate export earnings, but that the extent of such taxation increases as domestic sales rise. This provides a strong disincentive for software companies to address the domestic market, which in turn has serious negative long-run implications.

Second, Sections 10-A and 10-B of the Income Tax Act, which provide income tax relief to export processing zones (EPZs) and 100 per cent export-oriented units (EOUs), were extended to software exports from such schemes in 1993. Here again, software companies which have been in existence prior to 1993, and which form the core of the software exports of the country, have been excluded by oversight. As a result, the policy discriminated in favour of start-up companies and against established software exporters. Third, in 1992 certain specific software activities were declared to be areas of 'extreme focus' for export thrust by the ministry of commerce. In none of these identified activities India had any significant presence. Therefore, if this pronouncement was to be taken seriously, efforts at developing demonstrated competence in these fields in India would have to be taken up in a concerted manner. As yet no such plan of action exists, even on paper. These are only illustrative of the ambivalent attitudes that have characterised our approach to software exports. They can be multiplied many times over. It should not be thought, however, that the software sector has been totally neglected. In fact, the year 1991-92 marks a watershed in terms of policy support for this sector. The above cited examples are aberrations which have crept in primarily because of the lack of adequate communication and differences in perceptions that exist within the governmental system.

Until 1991 -92, there was virtually no policy support at all for the software sector. Even 'benign neglect' would be too positive a phrase to use in this connection. The primary vehicle of Indian software exports—on-site software development—was pejoratively termed as 'body-shopping' and every effort was made to discourage it. There was virtually no effort at understanding why software exporters behaved the way they did. In retrospect, considerable credit has to be given to the software sector for pushing ahead despite the lack of support from the government.

Since then, however, the government has taken a number of positive steps, albeit haltingly. Even so, there continues to be a lack of appreciation of the requirements for software exports in the wider government milieu. The popular perception appears to be that India already has all the ingredients for a successful software sector, and the demands for positive policy support are importunate at best. The real issue, therefore, is that whether there is any basis for this self-satisfied sanguinity that the Indian software industry will rapidly attain international stature without any active policy support.

In order to address this issues, there is need to analytically examine the behaviour of software 'exports from India'. The basic data is given in the Annexure. The time path of software exports in rupees and in US dollars are plotted. As can be seen, a substantial part of the reported growth in software exports has come about through devaluation of the rupee against the dollar, particularly since 1991. The decomposition of the growth in the rupee value of software exports in to the real growth measured in dollar terms and the exchange rate effect is given in Table 1.

The interesting point to note about this table is that the 'real' growth rate has actually slipped during the latter half-period in which the software sector has given rise to such strong expectations. It can also be seen that during this period, the 'real' and the 'exchange rate' effects have been more or less equal, which was certainly not true of the earlier period when the 'real' growth dominated. The differential performance in the two periods also cannot be put down to differences in the base, since the arithmetic mean of the growth rates of the two sub periods are not significantly different from the full-period average, which would have been the case if there had been a base problem

Casual empiricism based on this data and analysis would give rise to most disquieting conclusions. One would be tempted to infer that the software sector is starting to lose steam, despite the not inconsiderable growth rates that continue to be achieved. To make matters worse, this slowing down appears to have taken place precisely during the period when some policy support started being provided. This simply lends further credence to the proponents of the point of view which holds that software exports do not need such support, and more rapid growth is possible if the software entrepreneurs did not malinger.

In order to examine the situation in somewhat greater detail, an econometric analysis of the trends in the dollar values of software exports becomes necessary. Given the wide variations in the quarterly exports data, simple trend equations were not appropriate. More complex equations involving both intercept and slope dummies for the different quarters had to be specified and estimated for linear, quadratic and exponential growth paths. The results of such an exercise are presented in Table 2.11.

The results are extremely interesting. As may be seen from the table, until 1992-93, the linear trend equation is consistently superior to the exponential. This suggests that the decline in the compound growth rate indicated in Table 1 arises not so much from a downward shift in the growth path, but from the fact that a compound growth rate is an inappropriate measure of the true growth path. This is further borne out by the steady decline in the coefficient of the trend variable in the semi-log equations. On the other hand, it raises the question as to why the software exports followed a linear path in a world that tends to behave exponentially.

Since 1992-93, however, there appears to be a change, in that the semi-log trend starts dominating the linear. This seems to suggest that there is a substantial change in the behavioural attributes of the software export sector, and that the future growth may well turn out to be exponential. This possibility is reinforced by the robustness of the estimated parameters in the equations covering the periods 1987-93 and 1987-94.

However, on the one hand, it may be pointed out that the difference between the explanatory powers of the linear and the semi-log equations are not very different, and hence one cannot be too confident about this shift to an exponential growth path. On the other hand, even if the exponential growth path were to be attained, the annual compound growth rate has dropped sharply from 44.3 per cent in 1990 to 25.8 per cent by 1994. Therefore, what is the level of software exports that can be expected in the next few years.

There is of course no real answer to the first question, since the period available is still very short. Only time will tell. But the robustness of the parameters is an encouraging sign. The importance of shifting from a linear to an exponential growth path cannot be over emphasised, even for the relative short run. In order to fully appreciate the importance of such a shift, one need only consider the projected software exports over the next few years. These projections, both for the linear and the exponential growth paths, are presented in Figure 2. As can be seen, the two projections diverge quite substantially. In 1997, if an exponential growth trend is maintained, the level' of software exports should be about US $ 630 million. With linear growth, however, it is unlikely to exceed US $ 330 million.

**The Diagnosis**

The important issues that arise from the description of the symptoms presented in the preceding section may be summarised as follows:

*(1)* What are the reasons for Indian software exports to have followed a linear growth path? *(2)* What hope is there for permanently shifting to an exponential path? The first point that needs to be realised about the software sector is that it is not physical capital intensive, but extremely intensive in human capital. As a result, the growth in this sector does not arise primarily from investment in plant and machinery, as is the case with physical products, but from two principal sources: *(a)* The number of persons (or man-years) engaged in this activity, *(b)* The productivity of the manpower in terms of revenues per person.

**Table 7: Decomposition of Growth in Software Exports**

| *Period* | *Total Growth (PerCent)* | *Real Growth (PerCent)* | *Exchange Rate (PerCenl)* |
|---|---|---|---|
| 1987 to 1993 | 46.4 | 28.0 | 18.4 |
| 1987 to 1990 | 41.2 | 29.1 | 12.1 |
| 1990 to 1993 | 51.8 | 27.5 | 24.3 |

The exponential nature of most economic processes arises mainly from what Marx termed as 'expanded reproduction', or the process of cumulative accumulation of capital. In the software sector, unfortunately, this process has only limited applicability. Human capital tends to follow 'simple reproduction' behaviour. The reason for this is that the generation of the right type of manpower does not come about through the operation of normal economic forces, but as a result of deliberate decisions taken by the educational system. This is probably at the root of the linearity of the Indian software experience.

Although the Indian educational system as a whole has expanded quite substantially, there is a bottleneck at the institutions which are capable of producing software professionals of international standard for the kinds of jobs that are being undertaken at present. The available data suggest that there has been no expansion in the number of graduates coming out of these institutions per year for the past 10 years or more. This is a linear process.

Moreover, the Indian educational system has been most unresponsive to the educational and training needs of the economy. Although the structure of the Indian economy has changed quite dramatically in the last two decades or more, the changing composition of skill requirements has had very little effect on both the proportion of students in various disciplines and the curricula in the educational and training establishments. The net result is a growing imbalance between the demand and supply of different skills. The problem is particularly acute for sectors which are new and growing rapidly - like software. This strong auto-regressiveness of the educational system is probably the single most important cause of the observed linearity.

However, this is only part of the expiation. The failure of the Indian system is of a wider dimension. Despite the linearity in appropriate human capital formation, sustained exponential growth could still have been recorded through two methods: *(a)* Addressing more intensively those specific segments of the international software market for which trained manpower availability would not be a binding constraint in the foreseeable future, *(b)* Increasing the productivity of the scarce existing manpower by moving progressively to higher value activities. The fact that neither of these happened in any significant way calls for an explanation. The software sector can be divided into five major activities in declining order of complexity and skill requirements: *(1)* Project management, *(2)* Systems analysis and design, *(3)* Software maintenance and support, *(4)* Writing of code, and *(5)* Data entry. As things stand, the Indian software sector has been and continues to be concentrated in the second and the fourth activities, with a heavy predominance of the fourth.

Data entry for the international market is virtually

non-existent despite the fact that this is the one area where the resource endowment of the country is the best. The primary reason why no headway has been made in this area is the lack of adequate data communication facilities in the country, which causes long time lags between the receipt of documents and their supply in machine readable form. Also, correction of data entry errors, which can never be entirely eliminated, becomes more time-consuming and cumbersome. This has inhibited foreign clients from using India as a base for their data-entry needs. This is a pity since the data-entry activity, though low value in nature, is the one area in which manpower resources would not be a constraint, at least in the foreseeable future.

The situation with software maintenance and support is similar perhaps even worse since this is the fastest growing segment of the international software market. At present India has practically no presence in this area, despite its inherent comparative advantage. The primary culprit for this state of affairs is again the lack of adequate telecommunication facilities. This lack is particularly onerous in this sphere since software maintenance requires remote logging as a minimum precondition and customers insist upon the control that is achieved by on-line access.

The lack of high-speed data communication facilities has ramifications which go well beyond the restrictions it placed on the data-entry and software maintenance activities. The preponderance of 'on-site' software development in total software exports can also be traced largely to this factor. Indian companies simply had no option but to take recourse to this method of carrying out business. The end result was that not only did it increase the costs to the software companies, it placed severe restrictions on the nature and type of jobs that could be undertaken. Since it was clearly not feasible for any single company to send out large teams of software professionals for any single client, Indian software firms were limited to carrying out relatively small jobs or acting as sub-contractors in a large project.

What was much worse, however, was that it led to a gross under utilisation of talent. Since there was a restriction on the number of people who could be sent out, Indian software engineers not only did systems analysis and design, they also had to write the code. The latter activity is relatively more time-consuming, but requires much lower levels of skill. In most other countries, software engineers almost never write code. As a result of this pattern, Indian professionals have had to work well below their capabilities. Consequently, although the average salary of an Indian software professional is only about 15 per cent of an American counterpart, his productivity is probably no more than 30 per cent. Therefore, the real cost advantage enjoyed by India is not that large once this under utilisation of talent is taken into account.

The logical solution to this problem would be to have the software engineer doing only systems analysis and design, and employ lower skilled personnel to do coding, at least for offshore jobs. This will no doubt happen in due course of time as offshore work starts to grow, which in turn will require the datacom facilities to be upgraded quite substantially. It will also require much higher degree of project management skills—which is virtually absent at the moment.

## Table 8: Trend Equations for Sofrware Exports

| | 1987-1990 | | 1987-1991 | | 1987-1992 | | 1987-1993 | | 1987-1994 | |
|---|---|---|---|---|---|---|---|---|---|---|
| | *Linear* | *Exponent* | *Linear* | *Exponent* | *Linear* | *Exponent* | *Linear* | *Exponent* | *Linear* | *Exponent* |
| Constant (c) | 6.496 | 2.440 | 9.469 | 2.620 | 8.482 | 2.504 | 7.076 | 2.720 | 5.968 | 2.731 |
| | (4.30) | (39.31) | (6.87) | (26.30) | (5.70) | (36.70) | (4.74) | (42.05) | (3.81) | (46.20) |
| Trend (t) | 2.440 | 0.096 | 2.008 | 0.071 | 2.106 | 0.077 | 2.250 | 0.060 | 2.416 | 0.059 |
| | (12.60) | (11.35) | (12.65) | (8.98) | (14.95) | (14.02) | (18.77) | (17.76) | 22.39) | (21.20) |
| Quarter 1 (Q1) | 5.234 | - | - | -0.153 | - | - | - | -0.302 | - | -0.299 |
| | (2.48) | | | (-1.07) | | | | (-5.03) | | (-5.41) |
| Quarter 2 (Q2) | - | -0.362 | - | -0.431 | - | -0.237 | - | -0.479 | - | -0.486 |
| | | (-5.02) | | (-4.91) | | (-1.82) | | (-7.66) | | (8.83) |
| Quarter 3 (Q3) | 3.008 | - | -3.473 | -0.458 | -5.152 | -0.383 | -4.844 | -0.572 | -5.252 | -0.555 |
| | (1.14) | | (-1.15) | (-5.29) | (-1.61) | (-5.23) | (-1.53) | (-4.99) | (-1.63) | (-5.48) |
| t*Ql | -1.638 | -0.042 | -0.882 | -0.018 | -0.735 | -0.023 | -0.656 | - | -0.761 | - |
| | (-6.22) | (-4.97) | (-5.91) | (-1.41) | (-5.49) | (-4.21) | (-5.72) | | (-6.63) | |
| t*Q2 | -1.057 | - | -1.091 | - | -1.117 | -0.018 | -1.110 | - | -1.143 | - |
| | (-6.05) | | (-6.36) | | (-7.46) | (-1.62) | (-8.81) | | (-10.29) | |
| t*Q3 | -1.788 | -0.066 | -0.737 | - | -0.455 | - | -0.467 | 0.013 | -0.476 | 0.012 |
| | (-5.23) | (-6.90) | (-2.36) | | (-1.69) | | (-2.08) | (1.84) | (-2.40) | (2.06) |
| R-Bar-Squared | 0.9495 | 0.9263 | 0.9236 | 0.9094 | 0.9359 | 0.9317 | 0.9517 | 0.9576 | 0.9597 | 0.9672 |
| DW-Statistic | 0.9892 | 1.7329 | 2.7800 | 2.6181 | 2.7412 | 2.7780 | 2.7236 | 2.7785 | 1.1734 | 2.7100 |

*Note:* The t-statistics are shown in brackets

Perhaps the recent tentative move towards exponentiality in software exports is due at least in part to the fact that the share of offshore work in total software exports has gone up to almost 30 per cent in the past three years after being stagnant at less than 20 per cent for the previous decade. On the other hand, the same phenomenon can be cited for arguing that some of the recent growth in software exports is only window dressing. The argument is that typically in on-site jobs, the costs incurred at the customer's location were borne by the customer and did not get reflected in the gross foreign exchange earnings of the exporter. In the case of offshore jobs, however, costs of hardware, data communication and even travel are built into the gross export value. As a result, the difference in gross earnings between offshore jobs and on-site jobs tends to be very high, although the difference in net values is probably considerably lower.

On the whole, however, the diagnosis is that the Indian software sector has suffered from both a limitation in the availability of skilled personnel and stagnant productivity. Some of the reasons for this have been enumerated in the above discussion, but there are many others which also have had a role to play. It is useful to discuss these at some length, since they point to a larger systemic failure and therefore highlight the need for much greater degree of co-ordination than exists at present.

First, the Indian educational system is completely outdated in the sense that the both computer literacy and algorithmic or modeling skills are virtually untaught except in the engineering colleges and certain pure science disciplines. In actuality, software development does not really require engineers, it only needs certain mathematical skills. As a matter of fact, professionals from non-engineering disciplines can contribute more to software exports, provided they are-given the requisite orientation in their basic undergraduate education. At present there is a programme to inculcate computer literacy in schools, but that will take another five years or so to fructify. Unfortunately there is no such programme in colleges. This needs to be corrected urgently, not only for the software sector, but for most modern industrial/service activities.

Second, the telecommunication system in India is still very voice-oriented, and there is a total lack of appreciation of the role and importance of datacom. What is worse is that although high-speed datacom facilities are becoming available to the rest of the world, intra-country connectivity is still quite distant. This has two major ill-effects. First, mom software professionals, including those from engineering backgrounds, receive practically zero exposure to datacom-based work methods during their formal education. Most of these skills have to be taught on-the-job by the employers. If domestic datacom connectivity is not available, the learning curve is perforce based on the relatively high cost international facility, which can only be used sparingly. This restricts the spread of such skills. Secondly, the hardware platform base of the country cannot be used effectively by time-sharing. While this may not be a serious problem for large software companies. Which have enough work on hand to fully utilise their hardware base, it is extremely detrimental to the smaller companies. The ill-effects are further compounded by the relatively high cost of hardware in India vis-a-vis the competitor countries.

Third, the domestic software market has been limited not only by the extremely high cost of hardware, but also by an unwillingness to pay for software. In fact, most major users in India tend to rely heavily on in-house EDP divisions/cells rather than on commercially developed software. The government is the biggest culprit in this respect. There is of course good reason for such behaviour. For most major users, it is cheaper to hire software personnel directly rather than bear the costs of the overheads of commercial software companies, which can be as large as two-and-a-half times the salary bill. This arises primarily from the relatively low salaries that are paid in India. In other countries, with much higher salaries, such behaviour is not optimal. As a consequence of this tendency, Indian software houses have very little exposure in carrying out large jobs which leads to both a lack of project management experience and a lack of track-record.

This tendency on the part of major users to rely on in-house software development has certain other dimensions which need to be noted. First, the existence of such units leads to a reduction in the trained manpower available to the commercial software sector, which simply aggravates the basic shortage that exists. Second, since most of these units are treated as providing service or staff functions, the software capabilities that are developed are rarely used to the extent possible. Thus the considerable project management and systems design skills that are generated lend to be wastefully used. Finally, since the 'make or buy' option is biased in favour of the former for the large users, the residual domestic demand is restricted to fairly small or intermittent users who cannot afford to pay anywhere near international rates. As a result, the price received by software houses on domestic sales is considerably lower than what they receive on exports.

Fourth, the software sector itself is weak in many respects. A dominant characteristic of this sector is that it has grown not through consolidation, taa furlough fission. As a result, there is neither size nor specialisation. Further, because of the relatively small size of the average software house in India, there is a lack of standards and inadequate use of software engineering tools, which affects the perceived quality of the product and thereby leads to an unwillingness to pay premium prices by the customers. To make matters worse, strategic alliances and networking between Indian software companies to leverage their respective strengths is completely lacking.

There is an interesting, and very damaging, side-effect to this lack of intra-industry alliances. It has been noticed that most Indian software companies claim to be able to carry out virtually any software development work, to an international market which is very aware of the importance of specialisation and core competencies, such claims are not only treated with skepticism, but in fact lead to a lack of credibility in and negative perception of the entire industry. The long-run damage of such loss of credibility can be immense.

Fifth, there is also a problem that arises out of the exposure that the average Indian has to international conditions. Certain types of software activities, such as telecommunications, transaction automation, smart cards, etc., are simply not addressed since the Indian software developer has not been exposed to these in any meaningful way. On the other hand, activities such as user interfaces arc culturally specific, and no meaningful developments can take place until the Indian developer is fully sensitised to such issues. This kind of exposure does not come about spontaneously. Either there has to be an extended period over which software professionals need to live in the target countries, or such applications should be introduced in India with the minimum of time-lag.

The long and short of it is that the Indian software sector faced and continues to face formidable hurdles in doing business, and considerable credit has to go to it for having achieved what it has. More importantly, it should be clear that although some of the problems are internal to the industry, most are outside its sphere of control.

### The Prescription

Having defined the nature of the problems being encountered by the software industry in India, the issue remains as to how to take this sector out of its linear trend and place it on an exponential growth path. Clearly, the strategy will have to encompass both the numbers and the productivity issues. A few suggestions arising from the discussion given above may be made:

(1) The need to reorient and galvanise the educational system cannot be overstated. Efforts like the department of electronics accreditation

scheme (DOE-ACC) for introducing minimum standards to private software training institutes, or the project IMPACT of the DOE for strengthening the electronics curricula in the leading engineering institutions, only address the problem at the margin. More fundamental changes are called for. It is suggested that a crash programme in computer literacy and software methodologies be introduced at the college level. Ideally, the curriculum of various disciplines such as commerce, economics, sociology, and of course the hard sciences, should be changed to give greater focus to generating modelling and algorithm development skills. This would probably be much more efficient than expanding the engineering colleges.

(2) The expansion in the international high speed datacom facilities that has been brought about and catalysed by the department of electronics (DOE) through the satellite earth stations of the software technology park (India) (STPI) and the 'time division multiple access' (TDMA) radio-links of Satcomm (India), is only a drop in the ocean. This trend needs to be carried forward much further. The DOE facilities are limited by the licences that have been granted by the department of telecommunications (DOT), which restrict their operation to particular geographic areas and to specific types of customers. The bulk of the expansion will, therefore, necessarily have to be carried out by the DOT/VSNL, which bear the principal responsibility for telecommunications in India. While planning for the expansion of the high-speed datacom

network, it should be remembered that software exporters are not the only users of such links. Almost all commercial agencies which have international transactions require such facilities. Therefore, the minimum necessary expansion of the facilities will have to be orders of magnitude larger than the specific requirements of the software export sector. Unless this is done consciously and expeditiously, the infrastructure will get rapidly overloaded and software companies will be forced to go back to on-site work as the principal vehicle of software exports.

(3) International connectivity apart, the general development of the telecommunications infrastructure in the country is of the highest importance, particularly with regard to intra-country networks. The role of domestic high-speed connectivity in providing a low-cost training ground for telecom-based software development methodologies and in leveraging the hardware base has already been mentioned. There is a further dimension. The real benefits from computerisation are realised fully only when computers get networked. This is the international experience. Therefore, if intra-country connectivity of reasonable cost and quality is made available, the spread of information technology is bound to go up substantially in India. This will create a domestic demand base for software, and enable Indian software companies to establish their credibility and track-record for addressing the international markets.

(4) The importance of enabling Indian software companies to establish track-records needs to be re-emphasised. This is one of the major stumbling-blocks in entering the international markets. In this regard the government has an important role to play. It so happens that at present the government is the single largest consumer of software in the country, but it actually takes very little from the commercial software sector. This may make short-run financial sense, but the country loses out on the positive externalities that are possible. The government should therefore start contracting out its software requirements to commercial developers, rather than trying to do it all in house.

(5) In addition, the government needs to provide direction to the organisations under its control. In particular, certain public sector undertakings (PSUs) which have strong software capabilities need to be encouraged to hive these off as stand-alone subsidiaries. Fortunately, this is already happening to some extent, even without government intervention. But more needs to be done. Once PSUs start this trend, it is hoped that the private sector companies which have similar capabilities will follow suit.

(6) The STPs were established inter alia to encourage synergy between small software companies and to provide common marketing facilities. This has not taken place to any great extent yet, primarily due to the existing preoccupation with providing the basic infrastructural facilities to

the software companies coming under their charge. In the long-run, however, this is probably the most important function that the STPs can perform, given the fissiparous and antagonistic tendencies of the Indian software companies. It needs to be carried forward vigorously.

(7) Given the large number of software companies in India and their tendency to claim expertise in practically all types of software, there is a need to establish a mechanism by which a potential customer can get unbiased expert advice about the capabilities of the various contending suppliers. Ideally this role should have been played by the concerned industry association, which has apparently abrogated its responsibility. As an initial effort in this direction, the DOE has established the Software Services Support and Education Centre (SSE). Among the various services that this centre is supposed to provide, capability appraisal and advice is one of the most important. For this activity to be successful, however, co-operation of the industry is essential. Whether this cooperation will be forthcoming, or will require a certain degree of government coercion, remains to be seen.

(8) Finally, in order to overcome the lack of exposure and cultural dysjunction, every effort needs to be made to introduce the latest software technologies and applications in India. This too will not happen spontaneously. Deliberate efforts will have to be made. The DOE has recently sponsored a Centre for the Diffusion of

Information Technology (C-DIT), which is meant to focus on these issues. Until this process is fully under way, however, on-site software development and body-shopping will remain the principal vehicles for acculturisation of Indian software professionals, and care should be taken that unnecessary hurdles are not placed in the way of these activities.

## Annexure: Exports of Software from India

| Year | | Rs Crore | | | Ex Rate (Rs/$) | S Mills | | |
|---|---|---|---|---|---|---|---|---|
| | | Quarter | Cal Year | Fin Year | | Quarter | Cal Year | Fin Year |
| 1987 | 1 | 16 | - | - | 13 | 12.08 | - | - |
| | 2 | 14 | - | - | 13.4 | 10.22 | - | - |
| | 3 | 18 | - | - | 13.8 | 12.68 | - | - |
| | 4 | 24 | 71 | - | 14.4 | 16.39 | 51.37 | |
| 1988 | 1 | 24 | - | 78 | 14.8 | 15.95 | - | 55.2 |
| | 2 | 20 | - | - | 15.1 | 13.18 | - | - |
| | 3 | 18 | - | - | 15.4 | 11.62 | - | - |
| | 4 | 40 | 101 | - | 15.6 | 25.38 | 66.13 | - |
| 1989 | 1 | 32 | - | 109 | 16.0 | 19.88 | - | 70.0 |
| | 2 | 34 | - | - | 16.3 | 21.10 | - | - |
| | 3 | 30 | - | - | 16.6 | 17.89 | - | - |
| | 4 | 61 | 157 | - | 16.9 | 36.15 | 95.02 | - |
| 1990 | 1 | 37 | - | 162 | 17.1 | 21.46 | - | 96.6 |
| | 2 | 38 | - | - | 17.7 | 21.47 | - | - |

| | | | | | | | | |
|---|---|---|---|---|---|---|---|---|
| | 3 | 50 | - | - | 18.2 | 27.53 | - | - |
| | 4 | 75 | 200 | - | 18.8 | 40.00 | 110.46 | - |
| 1991 | 1 | 59 | - | 222 | 19.5 | 30.15 | - | 119.1 |
| | 2 | 53 | - | - | 20.5 | 25.90 | - | - |
| | 3 | 91 | - | - | 24.0 | 37.75 | - | - |
| | 4 | 128 | 330 | - | 25.0 | 51.00 | 144.81 | - |
| 1992 | 1 | 104 | - | 376 | 25.0 | 41.76 | - | 156.4 |
| | 2 | 94 | - | - | 28.0 | 33.46 | - | - |
| | 3 | 126 | - | - | 28.0 | 45.00 | - | - |
| | 4 | 176 | 500 | - | 28.0 | 62.82 | 183.05 | - |
| 2003 | 1 | 146 | - | 542 | 28.0 | 52.14 | - | 193.0 |
| | 2 | 131 | - | - | 31.3 | 41.85 | - | - |
| | 3 | 176 | - | - | 31.3 | 56.23 | - | - |
| | 4 | 247 | 700 | - | 31.3 | 78.91 | 229.14 | - |

*Source:* DBID, Department of Electronics, Government of India.

# 3

# *Relative Performance Differences Among Public, Joint and Private Sectors in Indian Industry*

## Introduction

Statements of disquiet about the performance of the government-owned sector of Indian industry are common-place, and major concerns have been expressed both by writers who have been senior policy-makers [Bhoothalingam 1993; Jalan 1991; Marathe 1989] and by academics [Bardhan 1984; Bhagwati 1993]. Yet, the extant comparative evidence that exists [Bhaya 1990; Jha and Sahni 1992; Ramaswamy and Renforth 1994] points to no significant differences in the performance of private versus state-owned firms. What is the true picture? The demise of command-style economies is already being attributed to behavioural issues that arise when government is the primary owner of enterprises [Roemer 1993]. Based on this premise, major reforms are taking place in most erstwhile command economies, and there is an explicit acknowledgement that private ownership will yield greater efficiencies and breed industrial success. If the Indian government-owned sector is, indeed, as efficient as the private sector, then the large amount of effort being currently devoted to privatisation and reforms is of no avail, since the efficiency gains are unlikely to be material. Conversely, the authors noted above may have substantive reasons for expressions of their disquiet, and contemporary empirical research could well be flawed. The resolution of such an important conundrum, then, has to be based on facts and evidence, and this paper reports the results of a study evaluating comparative efficiency patterns among segments of Indian industry owned by different categories of investors.

In India contributors to the equity capital of enterprises include the central government, governments of the various states in the Indian union, private investors and governments jointly, and private investors alone. The primary way to distinguish between ownership categories is to classify them as the state-owned (public) and the private sectors. The term state-owned is used in the Indian context to include enterprises owned both by the central government and by the governments of the various states that form part of the Indian union. The latter are called state government-owned enterprises. In subsequent empirical analysis, central government-owned and state government-owned enterprises' data are separated for efficiency estimation purposes. Though the term enterprises is used throughout the paper, analysis is carried out using aggregate data, as described in a later section of the paper.

Comparative efficiency assessment is also important for another reason. Research shows that the evolution of modern industry, the capabilities developed within industry, and the efficiency with which these capabilities have been utilised have been a major force in shaping the growth and economic strength of modern nations [Chandler 1993]. The state-owned sector accounts for a substantial part of employment and capital investment in many developed as well as developing nations. Therefore, understanding whether the state-owned sector performs better or worse than private enterprises, in circumstances where the state-owned sector is a major player in the industrial arena, is relevant in shedding light on whether national progress is being propelled forward, being sustained or impeded.

It is argued that the comparative assessment of state-owned enterprises with other types of enterprises is not feasible because profitability review of state-owned enterprises ignores the socio-economic objectives associated with state-owned enterprises [Bhaya 1990]. Yet, for a fundamental reason, comparative efficiency analysis matters. Industrial progress is determined not only by the rate of expansion of resources employed, but by the way resources have been utilised and efficiency in resource utilisation is well-acknowledged to be more critical to economic welfare than allocative efficiencies.

The Indian experience with the state-owned sector provides a rich backdrop for assessing comparative efficiency. In terms of magnitude, the state-owned sector constitutes a large proportion of industrial activity, and for the first four decades since independence the Indian economy has seen an ever-increasing role played by state-owned enterprises. Jalan (1991) notes that the total investments in Indian central government-owned enterprises was Rs. 1,82,000 crore in 1990, made up as fixed capital Rs. 82,000 crore, working capital, Rs. 76,000 crore, sundry investments, Rs. 11,000 crore and the deficit financed by the owners, the government of India, Rs. 13,000 crore. These figures excluded the assets of enterprises in the banking and insurance sectors, as well as those of departmental undertakings such as railways, posts and a large portion of the telecommunications network.

Table 1 gives an indication of the increasing role of the state-owned sector in India's economy. It shows the composition of employment, productive capital (including fixed and working capital) and value added between the state-owned sector (owned by the central government and various state governments), the joint sector and the private sector for six recent time-periods: 1973-74, 1976-77, 1979-80, 1982-83, 1985-86 and 1988-89.

With respect to employment, the share of the state-owned and the joint sectors has risen, in total, from 27 per cent in 1973-74 to 37 per cent in 1988-89. With respect to productive capital invested, the share of the state-owned and joint sectors was over half, at 58 per cent, in 1973-74. By 1979-80, this share had risen to 68 per cent. Though fluctuations have occurred, in 1988-89 the share remained at 66 per cent, implying that two-thirds of the capital invested in Indian industry is owned by the state-owned and joint sectors. Marathe (1989) also notes how there were less than five central government-owned enterprises in 1950-51. Ten years later there were 48. By 1971-72 there were over a 100 such enterprises and by 1980-81 the number has increased to 187. Currently, there are almost 250 such enterprises.

The paper evolves as follows. In Section II theory and evidence with respect to performance assessment are discussed. Thereafter, in Section III the empirical analyses are described. Data and estimation issues connected with the paper are discussed. The analysis is based on a comparison of efficiency patterns for 16 time-periods between 1973-74 and 1988-89, which is the last year for which data have been released by the Central Statistical Organisation of the Government of India, for four sectors of Indian industry in respect of which data have been reported by ownership type. These are: the central government-owned sector; the state government-owned sector; the joint sector; and the private sector. Data are collected for factories belonging to firms in each of these sectors, and the factory-level data are aggregated for reporting purposes annually. The data-reporting and collection is carried out under the framework of the Indian Collection of Statistics Act of 1953 by the Department of Statistics in the Ministry of Planning. Section IV discusses the results that are obtained from the empirical analyses, and Section V concludes the paper.

**Theory**

Arguments advanced for the existence of performance differences between private and government-owned enterprises are as follows. To the extent that ownership composition varies, principal-agent issues arise [Putterman 1993]. Property-rights, which are rights over the enjoyment and disposal of assets, are attenuated in government-owned enterprises because a market for corporate control is absent. Capitalisation of the future consequences of undertaking specific activities into current share prices is inhibited because there is no public trading of government company shares, leading to a reduction in owners' incentives to monitor managers, and the exit option that can be exercised where there is a market for corporate control is, therefore, not viable. Consequently, there is a lack of capital market discipline to which state-owned enterprise agent-managers can be subjected to by owner-principals.

Next, an issue arises with respect to the fuzziness of owners' identity. With many owner-principals there are incentives to free-ride because any owner bearing the costs of monitoring has to share them with others [Ben-Ner, Montias and Neuberger 1993]. The ownership of state-owned enterprises is vested in individual government ministries and departments, which in the case is the owner on behalf of the Indian union headed by the president of India. Theoretically, therefore, this attribute ought to ensure superior performance, compared to the private sector, since ownership is not diffused among many owners but there is only one owner who can exercise strong control. However, the government department is, itself, an agency for citizens who are the de jure owners of state-owned enterprises. This means that the control of government-owned enterprises, being undertaken by civil servants, is vested in persons who are themselves agents monitoring other agents, and have no incentives for carrying out their tasks.

The consequences are as follows. As a collection of many principals, citizens face severe agency problems, and in a democracy neither have the incentives, nor can they find it easy to control state-owned industrial enterprise managers. Individually they cannot arrange a private portfolio of state-funded enterprises, to internalise the benefits of information acquired from having undertaken monitoring activities. Then, the very diffuseness of public ownership implies that citizens acting individually have small probabilities in influencing outcomes or expressing voice. As a result, state-owned enterprises effectively become proprietary organisations owned de facto by civil servants or politicians, while managers in such organisations know that they are free of both market discipline or sanctions from the ultimate principals.

With respect to the issue of public versus private sector performance, Vickers and Yarrow (1988) have argued that it is primarily variations in the nature of competitive regimes faced that determine performance differentials between privately- and publicly-owned firms. The argument is that forces of competition have a direct impact on the cash-flows of enterprises. Given equally competitive conditions, private and public sector firms face similar potential to lose or make money. Since private sector managerial rent-seeking, capitalistic behaviour or the exploitation of public sector firms' profits for private political gains are going to be possible only when there are adequate cash-flows, the greater the threat that forces of competition will lead to the dissipation of such potential rents, the better firms' performance is likely to be and competition is supposed to be the great leveller of performance between private and public firms.

## Evidence

There is some evidence which finds that public and private firms facing similar competitive environments do not display any efficiency difference (Caves and

**Table 1: Efficiency Scores for Four Sectors of Indian Industry, 1973-74 to 1988-89**

| | *Central Govt. Sector* | *State Govt. Sector* | *Joint Sector* | *Private Sector* |
|---|---|---|---|---|
| 1973-74 | 0.596 | 0.656 | 1.000 | 0.908 |
| 1974-75 | 0.746 | 0.474 | 1.000 | 1.000 |
| 1975-76 | 0.597 | 0.676 | 0.922 | 0.866 |
| 1976-77 | 0.613 | 0.256 | 0.815 | 0.952 |
| 1977-78 | 0.544 | 0.582 | 0.912 | 0.959 |
| 1978-79 | 0.483 | 0.726 | 0.888 | 1.000 |
| 1979-80 | 0.466 | 0.498 | 0.757 | 1.000 |
| 1980-81 | 0.474 | 0.447 | 0.731 | 1.000 |
| 1981-82 | 0.608 | 0.579 | 0.857 | 0.988 |
| 1982-83 | 0.671 | 0.620 | 0.888 | 0.952 |
| 1983-84 | 0.525 | 0.762 | 0.954 | 1.000 |
| 1984-85 | 0.555 | 0.657 | 1.000 | 1.000 |
| 1985-86 | 0.879 | 0.892 | 0.925 | 1.000 |
| 1986-87 | 0.819 | 0.976 | 0.984 | 0.998 |
| 1987-88 | 0.951 | 0.618 | 0.962 | 0.969 |
| 1988-89 | 1.000 | 0.787 | 1.000 | 1.000 |

**Table 2: Composition of Employment and Cautal in Indian Industrial Sector-Trends Over Time**

| *Year* | *Sectoral Composition of Employement* | | *Sectoral Composition of Capital Employed* | |
|---|---|---|---|---|
| | *Private Sector* | *State Sector* | *Private Sector* | *State Sector* |
| 1973-74 | 0.73 | 0.27 | 0.42 | 0.58 |
| 1976-77 | 0.70 | 0.30 | 0.36 | 0.64 |
| 1979-80 | 0.68 | 0.32 | 0.32 | 0.68 |
| 1982-83 | 0.66 | 0.34 | 0.32 | 0.68 |
| 1985-86 | 0.63 | 0.37 | 0.37 | 0.63 |
| 1988-89 | 0.61 | 0.39 | 0.34 | 0.66 |

[Christiansen 1980], or that given sufficient competition between private and public producers, and no discriminating regulations, unit cost differences are insignificant [Borcherding, Pommerehne and Schneider 1982]. The competitive forces approach also explicitly assumes the absence of soft-budget constraints, which as Jalan (1991) has argued leads to attempts to keep public enterprises for which euthanasia is the only solution operating with a variety of life-support systems. Hence, in spite of similarities in competitive conditions, the composition of the specific institutional environments that private sector or public sector firms are faced with may affect performance.

For example, there is the reality of the political environment surrounding government-owned enterprises. While citizens may have little say in the functioning of government-owned firms, government decision-making is surrounded by a constellation of interests forming specialised coalitions interested in government-enterprise operations. These actors include politicians, unions, trade associations and consumer groups who can pressurise bureaucrats into directing government-owned bodies into acting in manners consistent with their own special interests. While the distributional consequences of such pulls and pressures may often be positive, their impact on efficiency is likely to be negative because such factors do tend to make the management process in government-owned enterprises complex and unfocused.

There is a large empirical literature evaluating the relative performance of the public versus the private sector. Boardman and Vining (1989) evaluate 54 studies, of which six find the public sector to be more efficient, 16 find no performance differences between the two sectors, while 32 find that the private sector is more efficient. Many of these studies have compared firms undertaking specific activities, such as running airlines, supplying water or supplying refuse collection services. However, comparatively few studies have compared efficiency patterns among different ownership segments of the industrial sector as a whole for a specific country.

There are some exceptions. Boardman and Vining (1989), in a comprehensive study, evaluate the performance of 500 of the world's largest corporations outside the US for the year 1983. The companies they evaluate operate in the mining and manufacturing sectors, and belong to several nationalities. They find that, controlling for a variety of factors, joint and state-owned enterprises perform worse than similar private enterprises. In terms of their key performance indicators, joint enterprises are no different from state-owned enterprises, but relatively worse performers compared to the private sector firms.

With respect to India, three studies exist. These have used a variety of methodologies, data and performance benchmarks. Bhaya (1990) uses Annual Survey of Industries (ASI) data for the years 1981-82 to 1985-86. Calculating simple ratios of net value added to fixed capital, working capital and inventory, but ignoring human capital utilisation, he believes it is safe to conclude that public sector management efficiency is in no way inferior to that of the private sector, but the sector does perform worse with respect to its return on investment.

Jha and Sahni (1992) use ASI data for the years 1960-61 to 1982-83 for four industries: cement, cotton textiles, electricity and iron and steel. The latter two industries, they claim, are primarily in the public sector, while the first two are owned predominantly by private interests. The authors find no evidence of allocative inefficiencies in general, and each of them are relatively as efficient as one another. Ramaswamy and Renforth. (1994) use 1988-89 to 1992-93 accounting data for a non-randomly chosen and matched sample of 55 firms each from the private and public sectors. Using the same measures as Bhaya (1990), they conclude that managerial efficiency differences do not exist between the two sectors, though public sector firms are again found to be less profitable.

These studies contradict theory and belief with respect to public sector performance in the Indian context. However, each study suffers from biases which call their results into question. Bhaya (1990) uses very simplistic techniques, a very narrow time-window, and eye-balling procedures as analytical methodology to reach his conclusions. Jha and Sahni (1992) are more rigorous in their empirical approach, but unfortunately restrict their study to four sectors only. They also evaluate allocative efficiency, and no conclusions with respect to technical or managerial or technical efficiency can be made based on their study. Ramaswamy and Renforth (1994) also have a narrow time-window, their study suffers from the same methodological shortcomings as the one by Bhaya (1990), and also from maximum sample-selection bias. They non-randomly choose 55 firms each from the total population of firms comprising the private and public sectors, and, given the wide heterogeneity of private sector firms in India, it is easy to choose a number of private sector firms which are similar to their public sector counterparts in efficiency characteristics.

## EMPIRICAL ANALYSIS

### Data and Context

To calculate comparative efficiency patterns over the period 1973-74 to 1988-89, data generated by the Annual Survey of Industries (ASI) in India are used. The ASI data relate to the organised sector of manufacturing industry and have seen prior [Ahluwalia 1991]. The factory sector summary is used as the data-source for this study. From the data set. labour and capital inputs as well as output measures can be identified.

**Table 3: Descriptive Statistics for Efficiency Scores, 1973 to 1988**

| *Parameter* | *Central Govt. Sector* | *State Govt. Sector* | *Joint Sector* | *Private Sector* |
|---|---|---|---|---|
| Mean | 0.658 | 0.638 | 0.912 | 0.975 |
| Standard deviation | 0.171 | 0.176 | 0.086 | 0.039 |
| Coefficient of variation | 0.260 | 0.275 | 0.094 | 0.045 |
| Maximum | 1.000 | 0.976 | 1.000 | 1.000 |
| 75 percentile | 0.782 | 0.602 | 0.744 | 0.638 |
| Median | 0.992 | 0.924 | 1.000 | 0.999 |
| 25 percentile | 0.534 | 0.466 | 0.534 | 0.248 |
| Minimum | 0.538 | 0.256 | 0.720 | 0.205 |
| Range | 0.872 | 0.731 | 0.269 | 0.120 |
| Inter-quartile deviation | 0.956 | 0.866 | 0.134 | 0.044 |

**Table 4: Non-Parametric Test Results Comparing Pairwise Efficiency Scores Among the Different Sectors Period, 1973 to 1988 (Overall Period)**

| | *State Govt. Sector* | *Joint Sector* | *Private Sector* |
|---|---|---|---|
| Central govt. sector | 0.00<br>(0.96) | 3.41<br>(0.00) | 3.41<br>(0.00) |
| State govt. sector | - | 3.52<br>(0.00) | 3.52<br>(0.00) |
| Joint sector | - | - | 2.27<br>(0.02) |

*Note:* The test compares whether the row efficiency score is significantly less than the column efficiency score. The upper number in each cell is the Wilcoxon test z value. The lower number, in parentheses, is the p value.

The advantage of using this data is that information tor the entire Indian industry is available. This includes information on firms owned by the governments of the various states in the Indian union which are also substantial players in the industrial arena, and whose performance has never been empirically analysed. The characteristic of this particular data-base is that data are aggregate because of the reporting policies of the department of statistics of the government of India. However, the aggregation issue is unavoidable since information on a key variable, that of firm-level employment, is just not available for private sector firms. Hence, any comparative study of efficiency has to use a data-base such as this. Aggregate data also helps avoid any sample-selection biases, since data on the entire industrial population is considered for comparative efficiency assessment purposes.

Since 1956, every conceivable sub-sector of Indian industry has seen their presence. Apart from defence firms, traditionally in the public domain, generation of atomic and non-atomic power, manufacture of aircraft, heavy machinery, and equipment or Mil and sea transport arc among activities carried out exclusively by state-owned firms. At present, state-owned firms also manufacture products such as aluminium and non-ferrous metals, chemical intermediates, iron and steel, drugs and fertilisers, and are involved in diverse activities such as construction, engineering consultancy, farming, handicrafts retailing, shipping, coal mining, oil refining, commodity trading, and software consultancy. State-owned firms operate in many consumer-goods industries such as condoms, hotels, handicraft retailing, food products, televisions and consumer electronics where competition among players is very high, and in general are subject to the same institutional and regulatory forces that private firms have to face with regard to day-to-day operations. Data for firms undertaking these activities are included within the data that are analysed.

Three inputs and one output arc used in the computation of an efficiency index for each observation. The inputs are rupee values of fixed and working capital, and the actual number of staff employed. The output variable is net value added, expressed in crore or rupees which is a standard measure of firm-level output [Jackson and Palmer 1988]. In the contemporary literature on efficiency measurement both value added and gross output are concomitantly used to measure output. However, Griliches and Ringstad (1971) advance arguments in favour of using value added because it facilitates comparison of results for firms which may be heterogeneous in material consumption. Second, inclusion of material as an input may lead to the problem that all variation in efficiency may be captured by materials consumption, thus obscuring the role of physical and human capital utilisation.

A further choice arises between the use of either gross or net value added as the output measure. Denison (1974) makes a case for the use of net value added on theoretical grounds by arguing that, since gross value added includes a measure of capital consumption, there is no rationale as to why capital consumption ought to be maximised rather than minimised. Nevertheless, value added captures hybrid aspects of firms' activities, as Diewer (1978) has noted. First, it captures a production relationship between primary factors and output. This relationship is based on managements' capabilities. Second, it also captures a profit-generating relationship between firm-specific capital and firms' output, which, while also dependent on endogenous management capabilities, is highly dependent on exogenous demand and supply conditions, since these conditions determine the prices a firm is able to charge for its outputs. In the context of state-owned firms in developing countries, administered price regimes may he in operation, and governments use state-owned firms to operate as indirect tax collectors [Reddy 199()l. In the case of India, this is particularly true for state-owned oil firms. Thus, there may be a large element of windfall price-gains captured in the value added measure for each firm.

To create value necessitates acquisition and configuration of capabilities, which are encapsulated in physical, liquid and human capital. Capital inputs, both physical and working capital, are also expressed in crores of rupees. Human capital inputs are expressed in thousands of employees. To deflate variables expressed in rupees the wholesale price index is used; the capital inputs and the output values are then expressed in constant rupees.

Capital inputs can be book-values of physical capita] given in ASI data, however, in measuring capital input, the use of undeflated amounts lead to inaccuracies. The book value series is deflated by price index. The weakness of the approach is that it does not take into account assets of different vintage bought at different points of time. Conversely, major lacunae of the perpetual inventory method, which can take into account the different-vintage issue, are the two key liability assumptions, for some base year of an amount as beginning capital stock, and an annual rate of capital consumption. Therefore, efficiency parameters obtained by different researchers can vary amongst themselves, because each researcher may choose to base analysis on idiosyncratic assumptions as to the base capital values and role of capital consumption

The ASI data reported by individual enterprises are collected at the factory level.

**Table 5: Non-Parametric Test Results Comparing: Pairwise Efficiency Scores Among Different Sectors Period 1973 to 1980 (Period I)**

| | *State Govt. Sector* | *Joint Sector* | *Private Sector* |
|---|---|---|---|
| Central govt. sector | 0.00<br>(1.00) | 2.52<br>(0.01) | 2.52<br>(0.01) |
| State govt. sector | - | 2.52<br>(0.00) | 2.52<br>(0.01) |
| Joint sector | - | - | 1.75<br>(0.08) |

*Note:* The test compares whether the row efficiency score is significantly less than the column efficiency score. The upper number in each cell number, in parentheses, is the p value.

**Table 6: Non-Parametric Test Results Comparing Pairwise Efficiency Scores Among the Different Sectors Period: 1981 to 1988 (Period 2)**

| | *State Govt. Sector* | *Joint Sector* | *Private Sector* |
|---|---|---|---|
| Central govt. sector | 0.14<br>(0.88) | 2.10<br>(0.04) | 2.19<br>(0.03) |
| State govt. sector | - | 1.68<br>(0.09) | 2.38<br>(0.01) |

| | | |
|---|---|---|
| Joint sector | - | 2.52<br>(0.01) |

*Note:* The test compares whether the row efficiency same is significantly less than the column efficiency score. The upper number in each cell is the Wilcoxon test z value. The lower number, in parentheses, is the p value.

For public reporting purposes, data classified by ownership category are released only in aggregate. Thus, for every year there are four observations with respect to output and inputs, given the existence of four ownership categories. However, time-series observations for each ownership category are available to each year between the period 1973-74 to 1988-89; thus, for each category there are 16 available observations. Pooling data by ownership category and time yields 64 observations to be used for comparative efficiency assessment. The ASI coverage and almost two decades of time-series data yields rich information on the entire population of enterprises that make up the organised industrial sector of India. The ASI has been carried out since 1959, and is the principal source of industrial statistics in India. The ASI extends to every part of the country, except some industrially-marginal states, and covers all factories registered under the Indian Factories Act of 1948. Essentially, all factories employing more than 10 workers and using power, or more than 20 workers and not using power have to report data. However, the ASI was not carried out for 1972-73, and data prior to that year is not available in collated form by ownership category.

The analyses involve calculating and comparing efficiency for the 16 years between 1973-74 and 1988-89. For each year and each ownership category an efficiency score is calculated, and to statistically assess performance differences between various ownership categories, the scores for each category are averaged for the 16-year period. Second, an issue is, have there been efficiency gains over time? Fundamental economic liberalisation started in India in 1991. However, there were two spells of liberalisation, one starting after 1980 when the prime minister Indira Gandhi commenced reforms, which her successor Rajiv Gandhi continued from 1985 onwards [Ahluwalia 1991; Bhagwati 1993). To test whether these had any impact, the growth rates in efficiency scores obtained for each ownership category are calculated.

**Estimation**

Data envelopment analysis (DBA) is used to calculate firm-level efficiency and measure slack in the utilisation of various resources. Charnes, Cooper and Rhodes (1978) (CCR) develop, and Banker, Charnes and Cooper (1984) (BCC) extend, the efficiency measure developed by Farrell (1957) using a fractional mathematical programme, where the ratio of weighted outputs to weighted inputs of each observation in the data-set is maximised. This approach proceeds by constructing efficiency scores for a number of observations. For each observation a single efficiency statistic, which is a ratio measure of performance as to how efficient each observation is in converting a set of inputs jointly and simultaneously into a set of outputs, is calculated.

There is now a large literature on DBA. See Majumdar (1994) for operational details and application in the Indian context, and Seiford and Thrall (1990) for technical details of efficiency estimation using DEA and exposition of details of the various models possible within the DEA framework. In extending the original model developed by Charnes, Cooper and Rhodes (1978) (CCR, Banker, Charnes and Cooper (1984) (BCC) show that the CCR efficiency score can be broken up into measures of scale and pure technical efficiency. This is achieved by assuming that variable returns to scale exist for firms and by adding a variable in the LP so that hyper planes for each observation do not pass through the origin, unlike in the CCR model where all hyper planes go through the origin because constant returns to scale are assumed. In the constraint set for the linear programming model, this variable is kept unconstrained in that it can take on values which are either negative (increasing returns to scale exist), or 0 (constant returns to scale exist) or positive (decreasing returns to scale exist) for each observation.

In empirical analysis using DEA each firm that is rated as efficient is used to define an efficiency frontier, and firms not so efficient are evaluated by comparison with hypothetical firm that is on the frontier, and which has the same output or input mix as the firm being compared. Then, the efficiency of the firm being compared is the ratio of the actual output levels to that of the hypothetical firm. For purposes of analysing managerial performance, the output of a DEA programme provides a key aid. The relative efficiency measure gives an indication of how well each firm is performing relative to its potential. Since the best firms have to score I, on a scale of 0 to I, the difference in scores gives management policy-makers an idea of the scope of improvement possible.

Within the DEA model two behavioural approaches can be factored in. A first assumption is that each firm conserves inputs; then, the algorithm evaluates minimal use of various inputs, with outputs generated kept constant. This is the input-conserving orientation. A second assumption is that each firm augments outputs; given a finite stock of inputs available, the firm seeks to maximise outputs that can be generated with these. The DEA procedure takes each observation's idiosyncrasies into account in the computation of its relative efficiency score. The weights that are used for each observation are implicit internal valuation schemes which are empirically determined by the algorithm, and varies from observation to observation. This is based on a determination of which of the inputs a particular observation is particularly adept at in utilising, or which of the outputs it is particularly adept at in generating, based on data. By assigning high weights to those inputs and output variables which an observation seems to be more adept at in utilising, or in generating, and low weights to others, the algorithm attempts to maximise the observed performance of each observation in light of its particular revealed capabilities.

To compute efficiencies and slack in resource usage, the BCC algorithm is used. One key output - value of gross output, is used. A better measure of output in efficiency studies is net value added. However, the objective of this empirical exercise is to specifically evaluate excesses in input utilisation and shortfalls in output generation, rather than measures of relative efficiency. There are a heterogeneous group of firms in the sample, among which the creation of output can be affected by several considerations. However, to generate output necessitates acquisition of firm-level capabilities which are encapsulated in physical capital, working capital and human capital. Therefore, three inputs are used: total fixed assets, working capital and number of employees. Firms which have a trading orientation are likely to have relatively gi eater working capital and manpower components, compared to manufacturing firms which have a high fixed capital component. These inputs can be combined in idiosyncratically different ways to create output. DEA measures how these input combinations are used by different state-owned units.

**Table 7: Sectoral Percentage Growth Rates in Efficiency Over Time**

| *Parameter* | *Central Govt. Sector* | *State Govt. Sector* | *Joint Sector* | *Private Sector* |
|---|---|---|---|---|
| Overall Period: 1973 to 1988 | | | | |
| b (growth rate) | 2.00 | 3.45 | -0.10 | 0.47 |
| | (2.04)* | (2.25)* | (0.21) | (2.41)* |
| c (acceleration trend) | 1.20 | 0.29 | 0.29 | -0.07 |
| | (4.97)* | (0.80) | (2.59)* | (1.38) |
| Period 1: 1973 to 1980 | | | | |
| b (growth rate) | -9 10 | -1.67 | -4.27 | 1.33 |
| | (2.98)* | (0.28) | (4.25)* | (1.70)* |
| c (acceleration trend) | -0.62 | 0.96 | -0.23 | 0.12 |
| | (0.41) | (0.32) | (0.46) | (0.32) |
| Period 2: 1981 to 1988 | | | | |
| b (growth rate) | 10.78 | 3.78 | 0.72 | 0.20 |
| | (3.92)* | (1.46) | (0.58) | (0.63) |
| c (acceleration trend) | 1.49 | -1.72 | 0.02 | -0.01 |
| | (1.08) | (1.36) | (0.03) | (0.60) |

* significant at p <.10 at minimum.

*Note:* Absolute l-statistics in parentheses.

## Efficiency Growth Rates

To calculate efficiency growth rates, an exponential efficiency-time relation is initially specified, as follows:'

Et = x (l + r)t μt(1)

which can be linearised as follows:

$$\text{Ln Et} = a + bt + \mu t \quad (2)$$

where Et = an efficiency ratio generated by the DEA programme for each sector and

time-period

t = time in discrete years (t = 1.....16)

a = In x = a constant

r = annual compound growth rate

b = In (1+r)

μt = In μt - IND (0,σ2)

The exponential form is chosen for the following reason. If progress is assumed to be dynamic, then efficiency in a given year is more likely to be at least a constant percentage of efficiency in the previous year and not a constantly diminishing percentage of it. The coefficient on time, b, is the continuous rate of growth, but given the range of values it closely approximates the annual compound growth rate, and the estimates of b are taken as the growth rates. A basic problem which arises in the fitting of equation (2) to the full time-series data is that the growth rate in a given period can differ from the growth rates of efficiency in the various sub-periods. The estimated growth rates in efficiency in each period can be higher or lower than that of the entire period, depending on the nature of policy regimes in place. Thus, sub-period growth rates in efficiency are estimated for the years: 1973-80 and 1981-88 separately.

The variations in growth rates shown by estimates of equation (1) raises an issue as to whether these rates are constant. Efficiency growth rates can accelerate or decelerate. To incorporate such possibilities and evaluate the rate of change in efficiency for the full period as well as for the two sub-periods, a log-quadratic equation is estimated, as follows:

$$\ln Et = a + bt + ct^2 + \mu t \quad (3)$$

A significantly positive value of c indicates an acceleration in the growth rate of efficiency; a significantly negative value indicates deceleration. The inclusion of time squares on the right-hand side in (3) introduces a multi-collinearity problem. This is solved by normalising time in mean deviation form. That is, it is set to zero on the mid-point of the time series. This procedure is followed for the full series as well as for each of the two sub-periods. This normalisation makes time and its square orthogonal. The normalisation of time only affects b. The estimate of c and its standard error are invariant with respect to the normalisation. In the log-quadratic estimation, the value of b is the same as in the log-linear model. The standard error of b is the measure of instability of the growth rate of efficiency. If it is assumed that the log-quadratic form is a better estimator of the true trends in the growth rate of efficiency, the instability measure of b is also improved, since systematic specification errors are cleansed from the data.

## RESULTS

### Comparative Efficiency Patterns

The BCC DEA algorithm, which makes no assumptions as to the returns to scale characteristics of the different observations, is used to calculate relative efficiency scores. The detailed scores for each ownership category by each year are given in Table 2. The descriptive statistics of the scores are given in Table 3, and form the basis of the subsequent discussion.

The sectors of Indian industry owned by the central government and the governments of the various Indian states have average efficiency scores of 0.658 and 0.638, on a scale of 0 to 1, respectively, for the period between 1973-74and 1988-89. Comparatively, the sector of Indian industry owned jointly by a combination of government and private owners has a score of 0.912. The privately-owned segment of Indian industry has a score of 0.975 for the same period. It is reiterated that these are comparative scores only. If data for later years are used, the resultant average scores may very well change. If a sector, say the joint enterprise sector, is dropped from the computations, again the relative scores may very well change.

Prima facie, the results reveal that government-owned firms are less efficient than firms in the joint or the private sector. The data also reveal that in the Indian context joint sector firms are more efficient than government-owned firms, but less efficient than those in the private sector, while the private sector is comparatively the most efficient sector of Indian industry. The variation in the patterns of DEA-derived scores are also of interest. The central and state government sectors have considerably higher variation in their efficiency score as compared to the joint and private sectors. The standard deviation (coefficient of variation) of the scores are 0.171 (0.260) and 0.176 (0.275) respectively, compared to standard deviation (and coefficients of variations) of 0.086 (0.094) and 0.039 (0.045) for the joint and private sectors.

Data on the maximum, 75th percentile, median, 25th percentile and minimum scores are given, and the range and the inter-quartile deviations for the four sectors reveal the existence of considerable variation in the scores for the central and state governments-owned portions of Indian industry. While the joint sector scores do not vary as much as those for the government sectors, they do vary more than the scores for the private sectors. The data shows that the range and inter-quartile deviation of the score for the joint sector, at 0.269 and 0.120 respectively, are higher than those of the private sector which are 0.134 and 0.044.

The greater variation noted in the scores for the government-owned sectors has a key implication. While the average efficiency of the government-owned sector is lower than that of the joint or private sectors, the scores have fluctuated considerably, suggesting that performance of state-owned enterprises has been relatively volatile. A glance at Table 3 reveals that the efficiency scores for the central government-owned sector was around the 0.5 mark during much of the 70s and early 80s, but rose considerably after 1985-86. It is feasible that after the installation of Rajiv Gandhi's government in late 1984 the liberalisation that was undertaken had some impact, and this shows up in the higher scores for the last four years in the present data-set. Comparatively, the portion of Indian industry owned by the state governments, prima facie, shows no discernible pattern in its efficiency scores for the 16 years studied.

Table 4 presents the results of a statistical test carried out to evaluate whether the average efficiency score for each ownership category differ significantly from each other. The non-parametric procedure carried out is the one suggested by Wilcoxon (1945).

As shown in Table 4, statistically there is no difference between the efficiency of central government-owned sector and that part of Indian industry owned by the various state governments, and the Wilcoxon z statistic comparing differences in average scores is almost negligible (with a p value almost unity at 0.96). The central government-owned sector is statistically highly inefficient than both the joint sector and the private sector (with the associated p values being 0.00). Similarly, the sector owned by the state governments is also statistically less efficient than either the joint or the private sectors (again p values are 0.000). Finally, the joint sector is also significantly less efficient than the private sector. However, while the efficiency difference is statistically significant, the significance is not as strong (the p value is 0.02) as it was with respect to efficiency differences between the central or state-government-owned sectors and the joint or private sectors.

It has been remarked that in the post-1980 period industrial reforms started taking place in India. Differences in scores for each ownership category are separately tested for the years 1973 to 1980 and 1981 to 1988 respectively to identify if the pattern of differences noted for the overall period stay the same in two sub-periods, one of which is pre-reforms and the other post-reforms. The results are given in Table 5 and 6.

The test results establish that for both periods, 1973 to 1980 and 1981 to 1988, the private sector is more efficient than any other sector. The joint sector is more efficient than the government-owned sectors, while being less efficient than the private sector. The government-owned sectors are made up of the central government-owned and state government-owned enterprises, and between themselves there are no performance differences in either of the two sub-periods.

**Efficiency Growth Rates**

The results point out that the private sector is more efficient in the Indian context, for the period studied as a whole as well for two sub-periods. Growth rates estimation help establish whether there is time wise increase in sectoral efficiency patterns. Estimates are in Table 7. In the period 1973 to 1988, central government enterprises' efficiency has grown at the rate of 2 per cent and the efficiency of those owned by state-governments at 3.45 per cent per annum, respectively. Both trends are significant; however, an accelerative pattern is noted for the central government-owned sector. Joint sector efficiency has not risen or fallen significantly, while that of the private sector has grown at a rate of 0.47 per cent per annum, a trend which is significant. A review of the results for the two separate time-periods reveals interesting dynamics at work. For the period 1973 to 1980, efficiency declined at the rate of 9.1 per cent per annum, 1.67 per cent per annum and 4.27 per cent per annum for the central government-owned, state governments-owned and joint-sector enterprises, the trends being significant for the central government-owned and the joint sectors. Private sector efficiency rose at the rate of 1.33 per cent per annum. Between 1981 and 1988, central and state-government-owned enterprises' efficiency rose at the rate of 10.78 and 3.78 per cent per annum respectively, while the joint sector and private sector efficiency rose at 0.72 and 0.20 per cent per annum respectively.

There are several reasons for the rising trends in the efficiency of the central government-owned sector. From the early 1980s, several industrial-sector reforms were commenced, and the public sector was made the target of policy-maker's attention. In the mid-1980s, a committee headed by Arjun Sengupta, now member-secretary of the Planning Commission and then economic adviser in the prime minister's office, recommended several far-reaching changes in public sector management and control practices. These were being implemented, albeit slowly, over the latter part of the 1980s and the improvements in efficiency bear out that they have had some impact in making the public sector more efficient than it had been, relative to its own base.

## Discussion of Results

The state-owned and the joint sectors account for two-thirds of contemporary capital investment in India, but are significantly inefficient compared to the private sector. If there has been a retrogression in India's industrial capabilities up to the 1980s, as authors (Ahluwalia 1991; Bhagwati 1993) have suggested, then the analyses carried out suggest that the government-owned sector must bear a great deal of the blame. The joint sector, however, is significantly efficient compared to the state-owned sector, and in India is an important player in the industrial arena. The joint sector consists principally of petroleum firms. Their performance helps to redress the situation towards ensuring the efficient use of public resources.

The results obtained have several implications from

the point of view of theory. Recollect that the DEA score calculated using the BCC algorithm is a precise measure of efficiency for each observation. In comparison with-the private sector, which is almost fully-efficient in a relative sense, because the average score is 0.975 on a scale of 0 to 1, government-owned firms are just about two-thirds as efficient, and these efficiency differences are strongly significant.' Ownership does strongly matter in influencing industrial performance in the Indian context.

Efficient resource utilisation helps generate surpluses, which can be reinvested towards the creation of further resources. Hence, improvements in efficiency have an impact on the future productive capabilities of nations by providing higher levels of re-investible surplus. For example, Jones (1991) indicates that a 5 per cent increase in the efficiency of state-owned enterprises, without any changes in prices or investment, would result in freeing resources of about 5 percent of GDP in Egypt, or reduce 50 per cent of direct taxes in Pakistan, or fund a 150 per cent increase in government expenditures on education, health, culture and science in China. The release of a similar quantity of resources can transform Indian industrial performance.

There are some possible explanations as to why state-owned entities show lower efficiency. They have been prey to inappropriate location and technology choice decisions, irrational product mixes, and imposed marketing arrangements. These decisions have been made for political considerations, and have not been based on economic criteria [Bardhan 1984; Bhagwati 1993]. As a result, few choices and incentives are given to managers to maximise economic residue, and neither are they accountable for attaining efficiency because ambiguous and non-economic objectives have driven decision-making. For example, in the Indian context these socio-economic objectives include the promotion of income and wealth redistribution, creation of employment, promotion of regions, promotion of import substitution, and being "model employers" [Marathe 1989]. Also, in the Indian context state-owned enterprises have been used to implement government policy with regard to stabilising commodity trade, or in making transfer payments to various specific sections of the community [Jalan 1991].

However, other key reasons as to why government-owned enterprises are likely to be less efficient relate to the type of monitoring managers in these enterprises are subject to. In the Indian context, government-owned enterprises are subject to the detailed oversight of the parent departments, as well as legislative oversight by committees on public undertakings of the central and states' legislatures. Therefore, the issue of ownership diffuseness is not a problem. Yet, enforcement of legislative committee findings does not take place [Chaudhuri 1994; Marathe 1989], and the disciplining hand of the capital market is also absent. Consequently, attaining efficiency is not a primary managerial motivation in the government-owned sector.

Second, the identity of owners is a factor arising from which government-owned enterprise managers tend to become agents without principals. Controlling-department bureaucrats, then, become de facto owners of such government enterprises. However, a major phenomenon to emerge in India is that of state-legitimised rent-seeking which has an extremely enervating effect on efficiency [Bardhan 1984]. For example, often the creation of government-owned enterprises has been driven not by ideological or pragmatic reasons, but to create extra-pecuniary opportunities for senior civil servants or politicians [Chaudhuri 1994].

For example, Marathe (1989:184) quotes B.K. Nehru, a former ambassador of India to the US, who has also held several key appointments in economic spheres, "It is simply that it has become common practice for public sector enterprises, particularly in the states, to be made into mechanisms to pro vide powerful politicians, who cannot be accommodated as ministers, with salaries, perquisites, patronage and opportunities to make money through corruption." Bardhan (1984:69-70) also writes "Senior appointments in the public sector are sometimes made more on the basis of political patronage than of merit (leading often to low morale in the ranks of the technocracy in the enterprises). Headships of public sector units, particularly under the slate governments, are indiscriminately used as political sinecures. Efficient managers who fail to satisfy the minister's political clients are often arbitrarily transferred". The impact of such a phenomenon is to create a cadre of managers in the public sector who are agents without principles.

Some authors [Vickers and Yarrow 1988] have argued that, given differences in ownership structures, the nature of competitive conditions faced is a key factor in eliminating efficiency differences between enterprises. The data, however, do establish that given similar competitive playing fields, institutional influences felt by the owners does matter in impacting performance in India. Such evidence is contrary to what has been established in the west (Caves and Christiansen 1980; Borcherding, Pommerchne and Schneider 1982). The fact that the public sector, in much part, consists of a number of private sector enterprises which ought to have been eliminated from the industrial landscape of India by selection pressures from the environment, is an indication of the policy malaises which leads the public sector to be appallingly inefficient.

However public sector management reforms, while they were started in the 1980s and continue to this day, have also had a major impact, as shown by the significantly increasing trend in efficiency of the government-owned sector in the 1981 to 1988 period. Therefore, in the Indian case it is not only necessary to continue with the major liberalisation to encourage industrial growth, but also to undertake speedy restructuring of public sector management and control prachces so as to continue the realisation of efficiency gains.

A key limitation of this study has to be discussed. It is with respect to the data used. While it can be concluded in the aggregate that government-owned firms consume a greater quantity of inputs, relative to private firms, in generating value added, finer analysis has not been possible. Within the data for each sector, say the central government-owned sector or the private sector, are contained information on firms belonging to several different types of industries. Data of finer granularity may reveal the specific industries in which state-owned firms excel at, or are particularly inefficient in. However, while key micro-level information may be available for one sector, such information is not generally available for other sector.

**Refocusing India's Competitive Advantage in a Borderless World Challenges to Corporate Sector**

We must define the terms that we are using in these discussions. By India being in 'a borderless world', is presumably meant that the import tariffs are at or are near the levels in other countries; that both imports and exports are relatively easy and not subject to constraints; that there is easy to low of money across borders; that direct and institutional investments also How easily into and from the country; and that India is a player in the 'inter-linked economy (ILE)' with a great deal of intra-firm trade. In this sense, India is still far from being borderless with the world. But we are today much closer to it than we were before, and over the next few years we will get even closer since we arc committed to bring down our import tariffs so that the maximum rate does not exceed 30 per cent (vs 65 per cent); and to mo veto full capital account convertibility in a few years. Our present maximum tariffs are higher than in almost any other country in the world; there is a trickle in relation to other countries, of foreign direct and institutional investments, though far more than it was until three years ago; overseas companies are beginning to buy whole or divisions of companies in India; Indian companies are looking at investments overseas and accessing overseas capital markets: there is a partial capital account convertibility since institutional investors can bring in and take out their money without any difficulty. We are no longer insulated from the world. For example, for the first time, a few weeks ago, Indian stock market prices fell with those of other markets in the world in response to a rise in US interest rates.

## Comparative Advantage

The other concept is that of competitive advantage which can be traced to the writings of Michael E. Porter. This is a refinement of the concept of comparative advantage. Economists have to a long time used the concept of comparative advantage to argue for more international trade. The idea of comparative advantage is that different countries have different endowments of the principal factors of production, namely, land, labour, natural resources and capital; and that these different endowments give them different levels of advantages in the supply of products and services. International trade allows a nation to raise its productivity. It does so by eliminating the need for producing some goals and services and by concentrating on those in which it has superior endowments. Porter argues that these formulation docs not take account of consumer preferences. Consumer preferences can be influenced so that companies are able to develop segments of markets and brand identities. Such market segmentation and brand development can give the company their succeeds, superior ad vantages compared to other manufacturers. Further, governments themselves can improve factor advantages through various schemes of subsidies, incentives, special depreciation allowances, cheap export finances, cheap land, low interest costs, undervalued foreign exchange rates, etc.

In past years, Japan and Korea have successfully used both routes to improve their comparative advantages. India tried the government route and in the process so over-regulated industry and trade that the results were quite contrary. With the new GATT

Agreement and WTO governments will find it much more difficult to artificially improve factor advantages.

**Restorations of Comparative Advantage**

In India, the concept of comparative advantage was distorted by a number of government policies. Concepts of monopoly or large houses, self-sufficiency and import substitution carried to the extreme, led to serious distortions in the economy. Other policies like Rupee Trade led to India exporting to earn hard currency, paying hard currency for imports and then re-exporting to Rupee Trade countries to earn Rupees. Export subsidies of various kinds made it difficult to see that India was the net loser in these transactions. Export subsidies which were to stimulate exports did so at the cost of domestic consumers. Import substitution policies and the craze for self-sufficiency led to uneconomic production which needed high import tariffs and to our producing inefficiently, in low capacity plants and at high cost. Low prices for some agricultural products compared to international prices, subsidies on inputs to agriculture, etc, mishandled resources so that we began to produce low productivity crops at high costs, instead of concentrating on those on which we could get better productivity.

**Competitive Advantage**

Porter has argued that international trade must expand, based role merely on cheap wages and weak currencies but because of productivity advantages in all areas. Hence, to understand "competitiveness at the national level... we must understand instead the determinants of productivity and the role of productivity growth"

(Porter 1990]. "Developing nations are frequently trapped in industries ... in which labour costs, and industrial resources are important to competitive advantages. Exports then compete on factor costs and prices" (Porter 1990). Competitive success depends on the competitive advantages which can be brought about by producing at lower costs and by marketing differentiated products that can command premium prices.

There is enough research evidence to show that India's productivity levels have lagged behind most other countries in agriculture infrastructure, industry and in many service industries.

**Developing Competitive Advantages**

Competitive advantage of all players in the economy, in every sector, can be improved by improvements in the physical and social infrastructure, power, telecommunications, transport (railways, ports and roads), housing, financial services. All these are inadequate in quantity and deficient in quality in India in varying degrees. The quality of human resources is not optimised because of poor food delivery to the poor, inefficient health and educational services, a practically non-existent social security system, poor nutritional standards of a large number, and inadequate training facilities in the various skills required to service a fast growing economy. However, even if these do not improve quickly, there are many things that can be done at the levels of the industry and the company which can improve competitive advantage.

To develop competitive advantages in industry we must have economies of scale and therefore go for larger capacities in manufacturing. Or we must master the technologies that enable low cost, decentralised production, with centralised marketing. In any case we have to produce efficiently, with high quality, and standardised products and services. Detailed industrial licensing, import controls, and government induced adversarial relations between small and large industries prevented Indian industry from following this route.

If we are to be competitive we need at every level in the economy, to: *(a)* develop new technologies which are not identical to those used by others; *(b)* develop differentiated products; and *(c)* Improve infrastructure resources so that there are no constraints on the developing of industries.

In each of these India has lagged behind in almost every sector of the economy.

**Some Pre-Conditions**

What are the implications for action, of trying to develop competitive advantages for Indian business? Some essential preconditions are discussed below. Vision: Each business must develop a strategic vision for the future, based on its inherent strengths. In the past many businesses may have been established on the basis of available industrial licences, or because there was a shortage. In a more open economy and with competition, "a business must have a well-developed and articulated picture of what it is about and where it wants to be in the future in creating sustaining values for the customer far better than those of competitors" [Ohmae]. Productivity: Each enterprise must make choices based on the ways in which it can improve its productivity. Some actions for this purpose, are:

(1) It must aim to concentrate on its core competences. This will mean divestments of unrelated businesses, and acquisitions and new investments to strengthen the core businesses;

(2) Prepare for competition in a borderless world (as of now, India is not in that situation). Even vertical integration of companies might become a competitive disadvantage in future years. For example, Henry Ford-1 had vertically integrated his automobile factory backwards to the point where he owned iron and coal mines at the turn of the century. The Ford Motor Company of today has found it much more competitive not to be in all these fields but to concentrate on the production of automobiles;

(3) begin to look at productivity improvements in relation to others not merely within India but outside India. Porter has said that it might be a good idea if Indian companies work on the basis of Rs 20 to the $ 1 and not the present Rs 31 or so, and on the basis that there are nil import tariffs so that the company can target to lower production costs and be really competitive under almost any conditions;

(4) begin to add value to resources in terms of people, technologies, capital, machinery, etc. This means investments in career development through training and job enrichment, participation at all levels, quality circles, cost improvement groups, suggestion schemes, etc. It means focusing on R and D, inventory control, materials usage, maintenance planning, etc. The business as a whole must look at every stage

to do better with less and this must be a never ending exercise;

(5) introduce new practices at work in all spheres of business so that people have more responsibility for their work. R and D: Indian companies have paid practically no attention to research, and rarely to development. They must begin to put in money into process and product development in order to upgrade both. R and D budgets must rise: use of co-operative and contract research must develop if in-house R and D is too expensive or difficult. The 1994 budget gives special tax incentives for private research contracted to public laboratories but has been little used.

In both 1989-90 and 1991-92 India spent less than 1 per cent of its GNP on R and D. This is lower than many countries, but given the low costs of scientific personnel in India, it still meant a large expenditure of Rs 5,141 crore in 1992-93. If we compare the per capita R and D expenditures in some countries in relation to India, they were

| In | More than in India by |
|---|---|
| USA | X 210 times |
| Japan | X 140 times |
| S Korea | X 19 times |

However, the expenditure on R and D in India in 1992-93 was mainly by

| | |
|---|---|
| Central government | 65 Per cent |
| State governments | 9 Per cent |
| Private sector | 15 Per cent |

Of the total expenditure, over 57 per cent went into space, nuclear energy and defence. The rest can be said to have gone into products and services for the market though it includes research expenditure on environment of 8 percent and on agriculture of 12 per cent.

The expenditures had little relation to the potential user of the R and D. There was little interaction between government laboratories, users and universities. Hence there has been little dissemination or conversion of R and D into new processes and products. Some attempt is being made to correct the institutional frameworks of government research laboratories and systems for recognition and rewards. Private sector R and D in many cases was really a name for the quality control function.

The fault is not that of the manpower. Very many high quality Indian scientists are doing extraordinary work in other countries, in many diverse fields. There are flaws in the way our R and D institutions are organised, good work recognised, freedom given to scientists to explore, and lack of intimate relationships with the user who must pay in advance for future results. These flaws have to be corrected.

Apart from limited R and D leading to little local process and product development, there is in India a preference for foreign R and D—and for technologies, products and processes, developed overseas. This is perhaps largely due to a lack of a successful record of work and is another argument for close interface between R and D and users. R and D must have an ultimate result.

*Joint Ventures:* Foreign investors in India were till

1991 allowed a maximum holding of 40 per cent in any venture. Many therefore went for Indian partners. The partners in these Indian joint ventures got to control the venture and the venture was the vehicle for foreign technology imports. The foreign partner allowed only limited access to his R and D work because he saw little reward and was afraid of losing his proprietary technology. However, the Indian partners who had the industrial licence did not in most cases do much to advance on the technology because they saw the licence as being enough to control the market in which there was little fear of new entrants.

As with cornering licences, companies cornered JVs for their technology collaborations. Unrelated diversifications with sub-critical capacities and technologies became the norm for many Indian industries.

Another fall-out of these joint ventures was that there are only a few major Indian brands in the organised sector. But there are many hyphenated brands—Merritt-Singer. Kinetic-Honda, Maruti-Suzuki, Shriram-Honda, Birla-Yamaha, Lehar-Pepsi. HCL-HP, etc. The JVs enabled MNCs to participate and understand Indian markets at low cost. It was a waiting game.

When the market opened up and they could take control, they had some knowledge about how to operate in India. It is not surprising, now that India is opening out, that MNCs are consolidating and asking for control or to take-over other enterprises and consolidate their positions.

The question is whether Indian companies should be afraid—or should they like the SSSs develop a spirit of enterprise among owners and managers of MSEs and LSEs? The answer is that all hope is not yet lost, but these organised sector industries which for years dominated Indian industries must change. Some ways in which they must change are described below: Focus on Manufacturing: In Indian enterprises, finance and sales were for a long time given special rewards—not manufacturing. This must change.

(1) Some instances of the neglect of manufacturing in Indian companies can be seen in: *(i)* MBA programmes, which emphasise marketing and finance, *(ii)* Production teaching is largely about operations research—not about manufacturing strategy, cost improvement, factor enrichment, etc. *(iii)* Many companies were set up with low capacities, based on poor technology, because of the licensing system. The limited capacity led to high costs. There was little development work, nor any attempt to upgrade products or quality. Some examples: *(a)* Our old fertiliser plants, *(b)* DMT caprolactum units, and *(c)* alcohol-based chemicals.

(2) The manufacturing company with good practices will develop much more intimacy with suppliers, and treat them as part of the company. The company's experts help their suppliers to improve.

(3) Indian industry and consumers take cost plus pricing as correct, and continuous cost improvement to absorb increases is not our normal attitude.

(4) Companies must re-examine factory locations dictated in earlier years by licensing but which

may be unsuitable for many reasons.

**Focus Products on Customer/Market Segments**

(1) Companies must focus products to homogeneous customer/market segments to give maximum satisfaction to customer segments. This will help to optimise prices and earnings while building customer franchise.

(2) The Indian consumer associates advertising and hence branded products, with quality. Survey data (NCAER-1994) shows that at the low levels of income of the majority, the consumer is willing to pay a little extra to ensure that he gets quality and value for money, but that he cannot afford the high prices of frill packed products which MNCs have developed as part of their global marketing. This is the challenge before Indian companies. They have to build production facilities to cater to these mass markets and to design products that these markets can afford. These products must build their brand identities and companies must find creative ways to do so.

(3) The customer is the one who pays the bill; not the bureaucrat who controls as in the public sector, or till 1991 gave industrial and import licences as in the private sector.

(4) If the customer is the focus—quality will be supreme. In India the customer has had no choice, voice or exit.

(5) But companies must aim to at least satisfy customer needs. They must, therefore, know

what the customer wants.

(6) The truly excellent company aims to delight the customer and give the customer more than he expects. We have examples of the last two in India but not enough. To be competitive, companies must consciously build the attitude of delighting the customer.

*Develop Brands:* Indian companies need to develop strong domestic brands and to target for a large domestic market base. Brand building does not necessarily always require large investments of money but understanding of the prospective user and his needs. Many brands that have been developed in India have shown this understanding, e.g., Nirma, Rasna, Vicco, Promise, Thermax, Bajaj; but they belonged to the small or medi um category of enterprise, not the large organised sector.

*Quality:* The truly competitive company knows that quality does not consist in merely getting ISO certificates from Bureau Veritas Quality International. It has to develop the ingrained culture that goes with consistent quality standards. Quality improvements are seen by many Indian companies as an additional cost and grafted on to the production system. But if quality is a core company value it has to be built in to the systems. There is evidence that a total company orientation to quality can in fact reduce cost.

*Indian Public Sector:* The Indian public sector works under the severe handicap of government ownership. This makes it vulnerable to many pressures due to ideology, politics, bureaucratic changes, and lack of commitment and accountability among government representatives. Labour in the public sector has much greater authority over management decisions and this is a bottleneck to improving productivity. Business decisions in competitive situations, cannot be taker in the open and be subject to public scrutiny. But the public sector has to be more open than the private sector in this respect. For all these reasons, improving public sector efficiencies with government ownership and control is a difficult task. The public sector in India if we include power, telecommunications, railways, ports, roads and posts is crucial to our competitive advantage as a nation. If these areas do not perform efficiently, the nation loses a lot of its advantage.

*Small-Scale Sector:* The small-scale sector is another area in which productivity improvement is difficult. This improvement is essential for improved national competitive advantage.

Indian government policies merely encourage the small scale to remain small. There is little automation, an inability to keep costs under control, and reliance on special preferences from government. The small scale accounted for more than 35 per cent of the contribution of the entire manufacturing sector NDP in 1987-88. Small Units are suppliers to the others. They are where workers in larger enterprises many times get their initial training. If this sector remains un-competitive and in continuing need of protection, it will pull the whole national competitiveness down. However, the organised sector can help the small scale to improve by partnering them, as has happened in Japan and elsewhere.

*Industrial Clusters:* Porter's analysis of the competitive advantage of nations shows that industries develop in clusters and these locational clusters enable substantial improvement in productivity, as units learn from each other and develop suppliers and skills in a synergistic way. It is not as if India does not have such industrial clusters. From the top of my mind I can list the following:

| | |
|---|---|
| Hosiery: | Tirupur |
| Textiles: | Bombay, Coimbatore and Ahmedabad |
| Brassware: | Moradabad |
| Electric Motors: | Coimbatore and Rajkot |
| Readymade garments: | Delhi, Bombay and Bangalore |
| Shoes: | Kanpur and Agra |
| Tannery, leather and lather chemicals: | Madras |
| Petrochem and plastics: | Baroda |
| Industrial chemicals: | Bombay |
| Software and hardware: | Bangalore |
| Gems and diamonds: | Surat |
| Powerlooms: | Biwandi, Surat and Ichalkaranji |

However, the Indian clusters tend to focus around large cities and towns. They do not develop in small places. The concentration creates major problems due to the clogging of transport and communication, and a breakdown in urban support system e.g., health, sanitation and water supply. The poor living conditions are not conducive to major improvements in productivity. With improved infrastructure these clusters could become important driving forces in the competitiveness of Indian industry. As a nation we must develop more such clusters in the country.

**Micro-Level Actions Required in Indian Companies**

As we move into a borderless world, our corporate

dinosaurs will become extinct. Many household names of today among companies and groups will disappear or become less visible.

In 1990 IBM had US $ 6 billion as net profit. Within a year, IBM, Sears, General Motors had become dinosaurs, companies which were stumbling in an unfamiliar environment, and having new competitors eating away chunks of their markets. Now they are restructuring to survive, and successfully so. There is hope for our dinosaurs as well but only if they follow the mantras we have listed. Who are our emerging dinosaurs?

(1) The unrelated companies that have diversified into businesses due to earlier cornering of industrial licences and foreign collaborations and who so went into many different product markets. They have to develop sharper focus. In a group of diversified companies, each company must have sharply focused products and markets and must have the freedom to function without the baggage of being part of a group of other unrelated companies in different businesses.

(2) Family-managed groups that continued 'chromosomatic management' when more competent people were available in the market. They will be overtaken by other companies run by professionals, whether from the family of the owner or not.

(3) JVs with foreign companies whose management control had stayed with local companies because of the 40 per cent limit on foreign holding. The

foreign holder will sooner or later demand larger equity and control over the business, or refuse to update the technology.

(4) Those set up to take advantage of market distortions, e.g., alcohol-based chemicals.

(5) Companies which have made little or no investments in continuing product and process design and development will be overtaken by those that are doing so. In a growing market, lack of growth will lead to death.

(6) Companies that give low status to manufacturing; cost plus enterprises; these include a large part of the defence industries, many PSEs, monopoly companies, e.g., Maruti with no other integrated car as competitor will find it difficult when Daewoo and Tata come out with similar cars produced in large volume factories.

(7) Private sector companies that thrived because their only competition was from PSEs and were able to stop worrying about customers, costs, and technology.

(8) Companies in sectors whose prices were controlled or administered, e.g., cement, vanaspati, sugar, etc, unless they learn new ways of survival, with competition and prices that are market-driven.

(9) Monopolistic or oligopolistic situations, e g, SEBs. executive in a borderless world

**Peter Drucker's Words are Relevant to Us in India**

(1) The individual has to take more responsibility

for himself and have less expectation that he will remain in the same company throughout his life or enjoy guaranteed job security. Therefore the post reforms executive in India has to manage his own career self-development through training and building experiences into himself.

(2) Education is not enough. The manager must develop competitiveness. Some indications of personal competitiveness would be

- Liking pressure
- Calm in crisis or confusion
- Absorbing information by reading
- Learning to quickly read graphs and numbers
- Alert all the time to any fact or data to see how it affects his work.

(3) He has to develop empathy so that he can feel people's problems and concerns and deal with them before they become articulated and serious.

(4) Develop self-discipline and self-control by practising yoga, meditation, regularity in habits, care in diet.

(5) He has to learn to collect, assimilate and find the links in information. Lateral thinking is a useful technique to learn, where he can make linkages between disparate facts. Therefore he must know what information he needs, where it is, and how to get it. No one else may be able to tell him.

(6) Become understandable; information must be

transmitted and stored if it is to be productive, not hidden.

(7) Team work; low brows must leant to work with high brows; not enough to be a specialist but need to be sympathisers of different fields of knowledge.

(8) Become executives not managers:

- Responsibility is for an area.
- Not necessarily dominion over people.

(9) Managerial change is required in Indian work ethics and mind sets.

(10) Indian executives must learn to become more egalitarian—ablc to do many things themselves, have more respect for others especially lower in hierarchy, because skills and ideas may not always rest with those in grey safari suits. They must learn to listen to all levels and not merely to the top, and to be less hierarchical.

**Conclusion**

India is still many years from entering the borderless world. Kenichi Ohmae described it as "the interlinked economy (ILE) of the triad (the US, Europe and Japan) joined by aggressive economies such as Taiwan, Hong Kong, and Singapore. For all practical purposes, the ILE has made obsolete the—traditional instruments of central bankers—interest rate and money supply. The traditional way of looking at trade statistics, based on a nation's balance with another nation have become obsolete, because ILE residents have learnt to move their production and other functions around." India today is much closer to this borderless world than it was in June 1991 and is moving with speed towards it.

In this new world that we are in and are moving to, we must aim to raise the competitive advantage of all sectors in the nation. This requires a different set of policies for government which emphasises removal of distortions in the economy especially in the shape of government controls and regulations that hide the reality of the economic situation. Physical infrastructure and the social infrastructure for human development must improve rapidly.

However, industry and individual companies can do a great deal to improve their own competitive advantage. These range from actions to improve productivity, brand building, emphasis on R and D as well as changes in attitude to the centrality of the customer and to focus on manufacturing as a discipline. At the same time, the large role of the public and the small-scale sectors requires that they also march in step and action to improve their competitiveness, is required. The development of industrial clusters is another way to get synergistic development. If these actions are not taken, many Indian groups and companies will not survive long into the new century. The individual executive also has to change if he is to function effectively in this new situation.

# 4

# *Financial Performance of Engineering Industry in India*

## Introduction

A close association exists between industrial growth and general economic growth. The speedy industrialization can be achieved only if the basic industries are suitably planned and started. The engineering industry products which includes the basic metal and alloys, metal products, machinery products, electrical equipments and transport equipments have to lay a pivotal role in this direction since they are the major suppliers of components for other industries.

A higher investment rate into the investment goods sector would mean a higher investment rate at the margin and hence a greater rate of growth of output. More steel per person means more machinery per person, and more machinery means more production per person (Mahalanobis 1955). In this context, the present investigation analyses the efficiency and financial performance of the engineering industry in Kerala for the period 1988-98.

The studies made on the industrialization in Kerala reassured the state's industrial backwardness but have put forward different hypotheses for this lag namely, labour disturbance hypothesis, wage cost hypothesis, psychic-cost hypothesis, Jajmani hypothesis and industrial structural hypothesis. The scholars who favoured the industrial structure hypothesis viewed that the slow industrial growth in the state could be explained by endogenous factors resulting from the process of development of industry in a lopsided structure rather than by the exogenous differences in resource endowment.

The hypothesis stated in the earlier studies which suggest that the inadequate development of demand based industries and capital goods industries (engineering) has led to the industrial stagnation in Kerala indicates that there is reasonable potential for engineering goods in the state which are now mainly met by imports. The development of engineering industry in Kerala is rudimentary and domestic demand is largely met by imports. It accounts for only 1.45 percent of the total factories with a productive capital of 1.03 percent, 1.30 percent of employees, 0.77 percent of output and 1.10 percent of net value added, of total engineering industry in India for the year 1995-96. Even though the engineering industry has to play a legitimate role in the state, it has not initiated the required role. But at the same time, even the limited supply is transferred to the other states mainly because the available designs are not in tune with domestic demand. In short, contradictions and mismatch are observed in the demand and supply conditions. This mismatch between the demand and supply led to the uneconomic operation of many of the engineering units. Even with much scope for the engineering industries in Kerala, the existing industries find it hard to grapple with many contributing factors that have affected its effective functioning.

Earlier studies on engineering industries are very rare of which majority studies pertain to aspects like trends and prospects (Majumdar 1962), export performance (Dinesh Trehan 1970, Sanjaya Lal and Rajiv Kumar 1981, Kumar Mahadevan 1981, Patibandla 1988, Lajpathi Rai and Janardana Sastri 1989, Sada Shankar 1990, Suvrathan 1991, Agarwal and Goldar 1990, Jojo Jacob 1999), rate of return (Ranjit K. Sail 1970), spatial dimension (Surajit K. Saha (1993) and linkages (Usha 1992). These studies examined the industries performance in the country and did not make any reference to its situation within the states. Hence, a study of the financial performance of the engineering industry of Kerala is essential. There is the need to study the industry's internal efficiency, which ultimately shall determine the overall industrial development in future. The present discussion therefore makes an attempt to discuss the financial aspects of engineering industry by analyzing the sample units consisting of four groups, viz., metal product group, machinery group, electrical group and transport equipment group.

## Objective

Financial analysis is a process of evaluating relationships between various components to obtain a better understanding of a firm's position and performance (Metcalf, R. Wand, Titard, P.L. 1976,). It is the process of identifying the financial strength and weaknesses of the firm by properly establishing relationships between the items in the balance sheet and the profit and loss account (Pandey, I.M. 1986). The objective of this paper is to evaluate the financial performance of engineering industry in Kerala to obtain a better understanding of its position and performance. For analyzing the financial data and interpreting them in a systematic manner, tools such as comparative financial and operating statements, common size statements, trend analysis, average analysis, ratio accounting and fund flow statements are commonly used. With this objective, the paper is divided into following sections.

## Materials and Methods

Engineering industry is primarily a metal using industry, though other materials like plastics, nylon, rubber etc. are also used as inputs. The industry includes the basic metal and alloys (group 33), metal products (group 34), machinery (group 35), electrical (group 36) and transport equipment (group 37) as defined by the Central Statistical Organisation. The definition of the AIE1 includes the industry 16 NSC groups. But the scope of the engineering industry in this discussion is limited to 4 groups only, viz., metal product group, machinery group, electrical group and transport equipment group because of the difficulty in perfect demarcation of the units.

The methodology adopted is both descriptive and analytical. Comparison of the data in the current period with those of the past years is very useful in judging whether there is improvement in the business or otherwise (Manmohan & S.N. Goyal, 1973). Financial performance is evaluated with the help of financial ratios and its consistency is tested using Altman's model. Judgments can be made only after comparing the trends or ratios with similar trends and ratios. But in the case of engineering industry groups such comparable trends or ratios are not available for the state and hence at the possible level the ratios are compared with the all India level ratios available for the engineering groups. This comparison of financial assessment, together with other efficiency criteria will provide a synoptic view of the total efficiency and performance of the industry.

The sources of funds of engineering industry include net worth, borrowings, current liabilities and provisions and sundry creditors. Among these the major sources of metal, machinery and electrical group to meet short-term requirements is the current liabilities and provision. The net worth constituted a major share in the total funds of the transport group. Share of current liabilities in the total sources of funds of the metal group increased from 51.30 percent in 1988 to 77.70 percent in 1998. In the machinery group current liabilities which accounts for more than 80 percent of the funds, increased by 147.06 percent over the period. Compared to the other engineering industry groups, the investment in the electrical group is very low. Current liability and provisions was only Rs. 35.55 lakh in 1988 which increased to Rs. 188.50 lakh in 1998 while the share of reserve fund and the amount in investors account was meager. The net worth which includes, amount of capital invested by the owners and the reserves constituted a major share in the total funds of transport group. Current liabilities constituted only less than 20 percent of the total funds. Table I shows that among the sources of funds the most important item in metal, machinery and electrical groups is current liabilities which consist of sundry creditors, bank loans and other loans.

Loans from banks constitute the major share of current liabilities in the metal product and electrical groups. In the machinery group, the major share of current liabilities is from the sundry creditors. It accounted for 94.17 percent of total current liabilities in 1988, but decreased to 80.28 percent in 1998. The overall increase in the funds from sundry creditors for the period was 110.60 percent. Metal product group was excessively depending on bank loans for funds in 1988, accounting for 92.33 percent of the total current liability, which declined to 79.92 percent in 1998. The dependence of electrical group on bank loans increased from 52.32 percent in 1988 to 66.84 percent in 1998. In the transport group, bank loans constituted 39.69 percent, sundry creditors 21.81 percent and other loans 38.51 percent of the total current liabilities in 1988. In 1998, the share of bank loans and sundry creditors increased to 42.69 percent and 42.98 percent respectively, while the share of other loans decreased to 15.09 percent of the total current liability (Table II).

**Uses of Funds**

Uses of funds are equally important like sources of funds because if the available funds are not judiciously deployed any firm may incur loss. The funds in the metal, machinery and electrical groups are used largely for investment in the current assets, which may decrease the profitability of the groups. Whereas in the transport group the major share of the funds is used for investing in the fixed assets. Share of current assets in the total investment of metal group increased from 52.21 percent in 1988 to 78.83 percent in 1998. The ratio of fixed assets to current assets came about 1:15 in machinery group. In the electrical group, current assets constituted 83.22 percent of the total investment in 1998. In the transport group, fixed assets accounts for around 80 percent of the total assets while the investment in the liquid assets is around 20 percent only (Table III). Too much of fixed assets may lead to a situation of shortage of working assets due to poor liquidity.

Current assets will be in the form of sundry debtors, inventories of raw materials, finished goods including semi-finished products, stores and spares, deposits and advances, cash in hand and bank balances. Major share of current assets is comprised of sundry debtors in the metal group (around 40 percent). The current assets in the most liquid form i.e. in the form of cash in hand and bank increased over the years in the machinery group and accounted for 68.47 percent of the total current assets in 1997. The share of sundry debtors and closing stock in the current assets of electrical group was 48.23 percent and 41.28 percent respectively in 1998. Cash and bank balances constituted only a meager share in the industry during the period. Major share of current assets of transport group was in the sundry debtors (39.28 percent) followed by cash in hand and bank (31.55 percent) and closing stock (28.07 percent) in 1998 (Table IV).

## Financial Ratio Analysis

The discussion on the composition of sources and uses revealed the broad trends. However financial efficiency, can be assessed only if we go for relevant ratios. Ratio analysis is a powerful tool for unraveling the underlying reasons for the financial structure, conditions and trends of business. Such an analysis helps in spotting reasons behind better or poor performance and in finding out significant derivations from any average or relatively applicable standards (Erich A. Gekfert, Richard D. Irwin, 1957).

**Liquidity Management**

Liquidity management of the four groups were analysed using the working capital, current ratio, quick assets ratio and turnover of current assets ratio. The skills in managing the working capital lead to the efficient use of funds and minimize the risk of loss. The working capital showed fluctuations throughout the period in all the four engineering groups (Table V). There are indications towards under trading and over-capitalization in certain years for the machinery group. The transport group has the lowest working capital directing towards the units inability to meet its current obligations.

The current ratio is the proportion of current assets to current liabilities. It a measure of solvency and an index of the working capital available to the firm (Sukla, R.C. and T.S. Grewal 1966). In all the engineering groups, the current ratio is below the standard level of 1.50 (Table V). This is a warning sign of insufficient resources available to satisfy current liabilities. The ratio is even below one in certain years. This suggests that the current liabilities are heavy and the current assets are not increasing in proportion to the increase in current liabilities.

Current ratio has the defect of treating a rupee of cash equivalent to a rupee of inventory. The quick assets or acid test ratio is a much more refined measure of the industry's liquidity. Generally a quick ratio of 1: 1 is considered to represent a satisfactory current financial condition (Miller, Donald L., 1966). The quick assets ratio was less than the conventional standard of 1:1 in case of the metal, electrical and transport groups. In the machinery group, it was around one during the period. Among the industry groups, the ratio is found least in transport group (0.57:1) during the ten-year period of study and highest in machinery group (98.6:1). When all the four groups are taken together, mean current ratio during the ten-yea: period is found to be 77.8:1 Thus this testing device for working capital position also point to the unfavourable liquidity position of the engineering groups.

The turnover of current assets ratio showed signs of improvement in the utilization of assets in recent years. The ratio was very high in the transport group indicating over trading of assets. The liquidity position as a whole was found to be more favourable in machinery group compared to the other engineering groups and least favourable in the transport group.

**Inventory Management**

Inventories are the stock of value of raw materials, consumables, spares, work in progress, finished goods and scraps in which the funds of the concern have been invested. Efficient management of inventories leads to minimization of cost of production, efficiency in their use and in maximization of owner's wealth. The effectiveness of inventory management can be measured by the ratio of inventory to current assets. There exists similarity in the fluctuations seen in the inventory to current assets for metal, machinery and transport groups. Among the engineering groups the ratio is the highest in the transport group (Table VII). It was not due to the over stock of goods, but due to the low investment in current assets which led to an unfavourable liquidity position also.

**Cash Management**

The objective of cash management is to make the most effective use of funds and to accelerate the inflow and decelerate the outflow of cash. A high cash balance ensures prompt payment but adversely affects profitability. Ratio of cash to current assets gives an idea regarding current operation of the business. In the metal product group, the ratio was high in the earlier years with about 59 percent 1990, but declined later and was only 18 percent in 1998. In the machinery group, the percent of cash balances increased from 33.9 percent in 1988 to 73 percent in 1995 and later decreased to 60 percent in 1998. Changes in the ratio for different years are due to the changes in the call deposits. High liquidity was maintained in both metal and machinery groups since they purchase raw materials by paying ready cash. In the electrical group the ratio was 4 percent in 1988 and remained marginal in late 1990s. The ratio in transport group increased from 0.17 in 1988 to 0.32 in 1998. In 1998 the cash and bank balances increased four times over the previous year, leading to an increase in the ratio to 32 percent. High cash balance ensures prompt payment but adversely affects profitability (Table VI).

**Operational Performances**

So far we have examined three issues relating to the performance of an organization which includes liquidity management, inventory management and cash management. Next component, operational performance will reveal the total health of a firm and also its capacity to perform day-to-day operations and make profit. For this purpose three ratios are computed namely, gross profit ratio, operating ratio and bifurcated operating ratio. Analyzing the figures contained in the financial statements we can expose the strengths and weaknesses of a business undertaking.

The gross profit ratio, operating profit ratio and the bifurcated operating profit ratio reveal the total health of a firm and also its capacity to undertake day to day transactions and make profit. Gross Profit Ratio shows the efficiency of the firm in producing and selling its products. It indicates the degree to which selling prices of goods per unit may decline without resulting in losses on operations for the firm. Even though there is no rigid standard to this ratio, normally 25 percent to 30 percent margin is anticipated. Over the years the gross profit ratio declined in the metal group and electrical group that too from a favourable position (Table VII). The low gross profit ratio in the engineering industry groups for various years indicate unfavourable purchasing and mark up policies, the instability of management to develop sales volume, marked reduction in selling prices not accompanied by proportionate decrease in cost of goods, unfavourable property locations and excessive competition. The mean gross profit margin for engineering industries taken as a whole was only 0.18 during the period. This reflects the higher cost of production of goods sold due to the firm's inability to purchase raw materials and other inputs at favourable terms and inefficient utilization of plant and machinery.

The operational ratio expresses the relationship between cost of goods sold and other operating expenses to sales. For manufacturing concerns, operating ratio is expected to touch a level of 75 percent to 85 percent. Operating ratio is higher than the standard value in certain years for the metal product, machinery and electrical groups. This is less favourable because it would leave a smaller margin to meet interest dividends and other corporate needs which may be the result of increased investment in current assets explained earlier. In the transport group the ratio ranged between 71 percent and 89 percent and ascertains the operational efficiency of the management in their business operations.

At the all India level, all the profitability ratios decreased in the metal product group in the years 1995-96 and 1997-98 (Table IX). This was because of the negative growth rate of profit. With regard to the profitability of industry, the situation of machinery group seems to be better compared to the other engineering groups in all India, while in Kerala it is the transport group that has better profitability ratios.

The disaggregate analysis of operating ratio further ascertained the influence of raw material on output (Table 8). The ratio of other establishment cost to sales was very low in the electrical and transport group. In the machinery group the operating ratio of both input cost and labour cost declined over the years. The ratio of labour cost to sales decreased in the electrical group over the years. Operational performance does not suggest a very favourable position except for the transport group. This may be due to the bad asset utilization or sales or both or due to other factors also. To examine this dimension, the extent of asset utilization with the help of three conventional ratios, asset turnover ratio, fixed capital turnover ratio and working capital turnover ratio were also attempted.

**Assets Utilisation**

The funds are invested in various kinds of assets to generate sales and profit. Normally the better the management of assets, the larger the amount of sales. Activity ratios like, assets turnover ratio, fixed capital turnover ratio and working capital turnover ratio are employed to evaluate the efficiency with which the company manages and utilizes its assets. The low assets turnover ratio in the metal product group shows a symptom of idle capacity or excessive investments. Though the ratio reported a fall in certain years it made improvements after 1994 in the machinery group indicating a tendency towards better utilization of assets. As a whole, the position of electrical group is seen to be better. The high ratio in the earlier years for the transport group showed better use of tangible assets but shooted to a value higher than the normal value since 1993 indicating overtrading of fixed assets (Table VII).

The ratio reflecting the fixed capital utilization once again ascertained the overtrading of fixed assets. The fixed capital investment was very low in the engineering groups except transport.

In the metal and electrical group, the working capital

turnover ratio increased over the years. This was the result of under capitalization and cannot be attributed to better utilization of working capital. The ratio declined in the machinery group after 1992. The high working capital turnover ratio in the transport group reflects an inadequacy of net working capital accompanied by low turnover of inventories and receivables.

The efficiency of the industry to utilize its assets at all India level was also examined using different ratios. From a healthy pace of asset utilization the ratios showed an unhealthy decline in metal group at all India level. Later on, the situation improved, but again it started declining after 1995-96 and the situation of Kerala was also not different. For the machinery group, though the ratio was high, it also started falling after 1995-96. The net fixed capital turnover ratio for machinery and electrical groups was greater than two during the period, indicating overtrading of assets. Similar is the trend seen in the machinery and electrical groups of Kerala. The ratios at all India level, in the case of electrical group were lower than that of Kerala, but the fluctuations in the ratios were almost similar. For the transport group the situation in Kerala is better than that at the all India level. (Table IX).

The various ratios computed revealed the trends in the financial performance of the engineering groups. The magnitude of ratios sounds to the financial health of the groups. But the analysis will be complete only when we make a comparative evaluation of the financial performance of various groups and make relative ranking. For this purpose various scoring techniques are available in the literature on financial management and the most popular is Altman's 'Z' score test (Altman. E.I., 1968) based on Multiple Dicriminant Analysis (MDA). An attempt is made here to estimate the score value based on the available data of sample units.

**Altman's 'Z' Score Test**

Here several ratios that significantly influence the health are computed and a single composite index, viz, 'Z' score which takes into account the weighted influence of different ratios has been developed. Altman's formal model was given by,

$$Z=1.2X^1 + 1.4X^2+3.3X^3+0.6X^4+ 1.05\ X^5$$

Where

$X^1$ = Working capital/Total assets

$X^2$ = Retained Earnings (loss)/Total assets

$X^3$ = Earnings before interest and taxes/Total assets

$X^4$ = Market value of equity/Book value of total liabilities

$X^5$ = Sales/Total assets

Z = Overall index

As the retained earnings for the different sample groups are not available we have not taken into consideration the value of $X^2$ while calculating Z score. In the case of $X^4$, we have slightly modified the ratio as Net worth/Total liabilities, because the formula developed by Altman in this regard is not suitable to Indian conditions on account of the underdeveloped nature of capital market. Besides the market value of the sample units cannot be found out, as they have not floated equity.

Values of 'Z' score above 2.99 are considered safe

while firms with a 'Z' 1.81 fall in the bankrupt zone, the range between the two values is considered a gray area. The value of 'Z' score reflects the state of health of the engineering groups and it also indicates the trend. Classification of the firms on the basis of the industrial ratios is given in Table 10.

The adverse liquidity position of the engineering groups was further ascertained in the model. The liquidity position is measured in the model with the help of working capital to total assets ratio. In the metal group, the ratio is very low (0.01) and remains almost constant throughout the period. In case of electrical and transport groups also the situation is not different. For the machinery group, the ratio is slightly higher compared to the other groups but still is below 15 percent throughout the period. This indicates that all the four engineering groups lie in the bankrupt zone (Table 11).

The ratio $X^3$ measures the operating performance of the different engineering groups. It shows how far the groups have succeeded in generating and maintaining profit. The ratio ranges between 2 percent and 31 percent during the period 1988 to 1998 in the metal product group. In the machinery and electrical groups the ratio was 14 percent and 50 percent in 1988 and declined to 11 percent and 16 percent in 1998. The ratio was below 10 percent in the years 1993 (6 percent) and 1997 (1 percent) in the electrical group. The performance of the transport group seems to be better compared to the other groups with respect to the operational performance, as the ratio was above 10 percent throughout the period and it increased from 33 percent in 1988 to 40 percent in 1998. Therefore based on operating performance the four engineering groups lie on the favourable zone in most years.

The financial stability is measured using the net worth to total liabilities ratio ($X^4$). The ratio explains to what extent a company is solvent to pay off the outsiders liability out of the capital employed in the organization. The ratio is below 50 percent all through the years in metal product, machinery and electrical groups. The groups lie in the bankrupt zone as far as solvency is concerned. In the transport group the ratio was 82 percent in 1988 and later declined to 79 percent and so it lies in the gray zone.

Sales to total assets ratio is a yardstick to measure the sales generating liability of the groups. In the metal group the ratio increased from 24 percent in 1988 to 170 percent in 1998. The group was in the unfavourable zone in the earlier period but it moved on to the gray zone in 1991 and later to the healthy zone. The machinery group moved from gray zone to healthy zone in 1990 but again fell back. The positive situation in the market and the steps taken by the management again led the group to the favourable zone after 1994. The ratio was above 100 percent in the electrical and transport groups throughout the period of study and hence the groups lie in healthy zone as far as sales generating capacity is concerned. For the transport group the ratio was very high after 1993 probably due to the overtrading of assets.

Applying the Altman's 'Z' test, the score increased from 0.76 in 1988 to 2.95 in 1998 in the metal group (Table 12). The ratio was above 1.81 in 1998 but still the group has not moved on to the safe zone. Except for the years 1991, 1997 and 1998 the machinery group lies in the unfavourable zone. The analysis of the 'Z' score of the electrical group revealed that the group was in the healthy zone during the earlier years of the study but later moved on to the gray zone in 1992 and to unfavourable zone in 1993. There were marginal improvements in the financial position of the group in 1994, 1995 and 1996 but again fell into bankrupt zone in the following years. The overall financial position of the transport group is better compared to the other engineering groups and the group moved on from a score of 2.93 (gray zone) in !988 i lower score of 2.21 in 1991 and later moved on to a score value much higher than the variations in financial performance of various groups of engineering industry.

**Conclusion and Policy Implications**

This paper has attempted to analyse the financial structure and performance of engineering study in Kerala and its four major groups on the basis of financial ratios and fitting Altman's model based on Multiple Discriminant Analysis (MDA). The main findings emerging from the foregoing analysis are as follows:

(1) The analysis highlighted the financial commitments of the engineering units. There is shortage of working capital, which has resulted in low capacity utilization.

(2) Receivables account for the highest share of funds in the engineering groups. This indicates the delay in making payments.

(3) The analysis clearly spells out that there exist idle capacities, overtrading of assets, inadequacy of working capital accompanied by low turnover

of inventories and receivables.

(4) Unfavourable purchasing and markup policies, the inability of the management to develop sales, marked reduction in selling prices not accompanied by proportionate decrease in cost of goods and excessive competition were also indicated by the trends in operating ratios.

(5) The trends in bifurcated operating ratios point to the excess influence of raw material on sales. Keeping in view these factors, the following policy measures may be adopted.

(1) Throughout the discussion, the financial commitments of the engineering units which adversely affected the financial performance of the engineering industry was observed. Hence the government and commercial banks may resort to various policy options to extend sufficient finance at reasonable cost.

(2) Adequate and regular supply of raw material should be ensured in order to augment the production. Since the raw material is not available in the state, the state government can wisely think of giving subsidy or other concession on imports so that the cost of production can be curtailed and thereby the large financial commitments.

(3) It is high time to modernize and update the technology of the engineering units. This requires finance, will and dedication from the part of the unit owners.

(4) One of the limitations of the state government is the lack of a perspective policy in all fronts where engineering industry is also not an

exemption. Considering the strategic importance of the engineering industry in the state particularly in the context of decentralization, the state government can appoint a task force for the purpose.

(5) Full utilization of the capacity in the units should be ensured. So far the capacity utilization could not be fully harnessed due to inadequate and delay in attaining finance. This has led to a high cost per unit of production.

It must be appreciated today that in the age of globalisation and free market regime, if the state is to emerge as a global player of significance, the flow of investment to this key industry has to be augmented to levels which are much higher than what they use at present. Liberalized policy should be aiming at the upgradation of the technology, thereby improving the quality and productivity in the engineering industry. R & D activities should be more intensified, which will enable the engineering units to go for updating their moulds and designs. Computer aided designs will definitely help them in this direction. The measures for cost control, modernisation, upgradation, computerization etc. will help in strengthening the forward and backward linkages of the engineering industry within the state. The industry must keep abreast with the rapid technological changes also.

**Table 1. Sources of Funds**

| Year | Metal Industry | | | | Machinery Insuslry | | | | Electrical Industry | | | | Transport Industry | | | |
|---|---|---|---|---|---|---|---|---|---|---|---|---|---|---|---|---|
| | Current Liability | Reserve Funds | Investors Account | Total | Current Liability | Reserve Funds | Investors Account | Total | Current Liability | Reserve Funds | Investor Account | Total | Current Liability | Reserve Funds | Investor Account | Total |
| 1988 | 81.12 (51.30) | 34.40 (21.80) | 42.48 (26.90) | 158.00 (100) | 119.23 (84.60) | 9.82 (7.00) | 11.80 (8.40) | 140.85 (100) | 35.55 (75.60) | 7.30 (15.50) | 4.15 (8.80) | 47.0 (100) | 22.93 (18.47) | 37.40 (30.13) | 63.80 (51.40) | 124.13 (100) |
| 1989 | 106.69 (53.IK)) | 44.30 (22.00) | 50.21 (25.00) | 201.20 (100) | 164.15 (85.40) | 13.15 (6.80) | 15.0 (7.80) | 192.30 (100) | 34.45 (75.40) | 6.20 (13.60) | 5.05 (11.10) | 45.70 (100) | 21.48 (16.00) | 37.22 (27.80) | 75.40 (56.20) | 134.10 (100) |
| 1990 | 135.19 (63.10) | 40.20 (18.80) | 38.70 (18.10) | 214.09 (100) | 155.64 (90.70) | 6.34 (3.70) | 9.63 (5.60) | 171.61 (100) | 36.53 (75,90) | 6.40 (13.30) | 5.17 (10.70) | 48.10 (100) | 27.81 (18.40) | 44.79 (29.60) | 78.70 (52.00) | 151.30 (100) |
| 1991 | 142.83 (67.00) | 33.50 (15.70) | 36.97 (17.30) | 213.30 (100) | 169.05 (87.90) | 10.39 (5.40) | 12.79 (6.70) | 192.23 (100) | 48.54 (76.40) | 7.52 (11.80) | 7.44 (11.70) | 63.50 (100) | 32.03 (19.90) | 49.87 (31.00) | 79.20 (49.20) | 161.10 (100) |
| 1992 | 159.09 (72.40) | 32.30 (14.70) | 28.31 (12.90) | 219.70 (100) | 245.71 (82.70) | 20.30 (6.80) | 31.01 (10.50) | 297.02 100 | 64.02 (82.90) | 7.31 (9.50) | 5.87 (7.60) | 77.20 (100) | 32.46 (19.50) | 53.23 (32.10) | 80.31 (48.40) | 166.00 (100) |
| 1993 | 176.46 (74.60) | 31.70 (13.40) | 28.54 (12.00) | 236.70 (100) | 276.60 (81.50) | 22.10 (6.50) | 40.65 (12.00) | 339.35 (100) | 68.42 (75.60) | 11.50 (12.70) | 10.58 (11.70) | 90.50 (100) | 33.48 (18.50) | 62.92 (34.70) | 84.70 (46.80) | 181.10 (100) |
| 1994 | 184.20 (76.40) | 25.30 (10.50) | 31.6 (13.10) | 241.10 (100) | 259.66 (84.40) | 22.93 (7.50) | 25.02 (8.10) | 307.61 (100) | 87.17 (81.90) | 7.20 (6.80) | 12.03 (11.30) | 106.40 (100) | 31.58 (16.80) | 58.92 (31.40) | 97.30 (51.80) | 187.80 (100) |
| 1995 | 199.17 (79.10) | 25.50 (10.10) | 27.13 (10.80) | 251.80 (100) | 205.62 (79.50) | 23.13 (8.90) | 29.95 (11.60) | 258.70 (100) | 117.32 (89.10) | 7.70 (5.90) | 6.58 (5.00) | 131.60 (100) | 33.17 (17.30) | 75.51 (39.50) | 82.52 (43.20) | 191.20 (100) |
| 1996 | 203.95 (77.50) | 27.3 (10.40) | 32.05 (12.20) | 263.3 (100) | 230.93 (82.40) | 23.68 (8.40) | 25.68 (9.20) | 280.29 (100) | 120.33 (87.96) | 10.50 (7.68) | 5.97 (4.36) | 136.80 (100) | 32.62 (17.10) | 60.38 (31.50) | 98.30 (51,40) | 191.30 (100) |
| 1997 | 216.85 (78.60) | 28.10 (10.20) | 31.05 (11.20) | 276.00 (100) | 247.96 (81.10) | 24.93 (8.10) | 33.04 (10.90) | 305.93 (100) | 164.55 (77.50) | 10.70 (5.00) | 37.15 (17.50) | 212.40 (100) | 31.68 (16.30) | 62.35 (32.10) | 100.17 (51.60) | 194.20 (100) |
| 1998 | 186.05 (77.70) | 25.20 (10.50) | 28.05 (11.80) | 239.30 (100) | 294.57 (82.80) | 26.69 (7.50) | 34.09 (9.70) | 355.35 (100) | 188.50 (81.60) | 12.63 (5.50) | 29.87 (12.90) | 231.10 (100) | 42.30 (20.60) | 63.7 (31.00) | 99.40 (48.40) | 205.40 (100) |
| Percentage change over the period | 129.40 | -26.70 | -34.00 | 51.50 | 147.06 | 171.79 | 188.90 | 152.72 | 430.20 | 73.01 | 619.80 | 391.50 | 84.50 | 70.30 | 55.80 | 65.20 |

Note : Figures in brackets give percentage total. Source: Survey Data.

## Table II. Current Liability

| Year | Metal Industry | | | | Machinery Insustry | | | | Electrical Industry | | | | Transport Industry | | | |
|---|---|---|---|---|---|---|---|---|---|---|---|---|---|---|---|---|
| | Bank loans | Sundry creditors | Other loans | Tola! | Bank loans | Sundry creditors | Other loans | Total | Bank loans | Sundry creditors | Other loans | Total | Bank loans | Sundry creditors | Other loans | Total |
| 1988 | 74.90 (92.33) | 0.90 (1.11) | 5.32 (6.56) | 81.12 (100) | 4.59 (3.85) | 112.28 (94.17) | 2.36 (1.98) | 119.23 (100) | 18.60 (52.32) | 15.3 (43.04) | 1.65 (4.64) | 35.55 (100) | 9.10 (39.69) | 5.00 (21.81) | 8.83 (38.51) | 22.93 (100) |
| 1989 | 97.97 (91.83) | 1.02 (0.96) | 7.70 (7.22) | 106.69 (100) | 4.97 (3.03) | 150.45 (91.68) | 8.73 (5.32) | 164.15 (100) | 18.90 (54.86) | 13.90 (40.35) | 1.65 (4.79) | 34.45 (100) | 9.30 (43.30) | 5.10 (23.74) | 7.08 (32.96) | 21.48 (100) |
| 1990 | 116.20 (85.95) | 8.39 (6.21) | 10.60 (7.84) | 135.19 (100) | 9.24 (5.94) | 137.05 (88.06) | 9.35 (6.01) | 155.64 (100) | 20.50 (56.12) | 14.20 (38.87) | 1.83 (5.01) | 36.53 (100) | 11.30 (40.63) | 5.31 (17.09) | 11.20 (40.27) | 27.81 (100) |
| 1991 | 123.50 (86.47) | 9.03 (6.32) | 10.30 (7.21) | 12.83 (100) | 7.57 (4.48) | 151.02 (89.33) | 10.46 (6.19) | 169.05 (100) | 26.50 (54.59) | 20.20 (41.62) | 1.84 (3.79) | 48.54 (100) | 13.20 (41.21) | 6.00 (18.73) | 12.83 (40.06) | 32.03 (100) |
| 1992 | 139.60 (87.75) | 10.30 (6.47) | 9.19 (5.78) | 159.09 (100) | 5.76 (2.34) | 229.54 (93.42) | 10.41 (4.24) | 245.71 (100) | 43.60 (68.10) | 18.02 (28.12) | 2.4 (3.75) | 64.02 (100) | 12.60 (38.82) | 7.40 (22.80) | 12.46 (38.39) | 32.46 (100) |
| 1993 | 157.40 (89.20) | 10.10 (5.72) | 8.96 (5.08) | 176.46 (100) | 6.74 (2.44) | 266.45 (96.33) | 3.41 (1.23) | 276.60 (100) | 42.10 (61.53) | 24.20 (35.37) | 2.12 (3.10) | 68.42 (100) | 12.90 (38.53) | 8.40 (25.09) | 12.18 (36.38) | 33.48 (100) |
| 1994 | 166.10 (90.17) | 11.20 (6.08) | 6.91 (3.75) | 184.21 (100) | 7.42 (2.86) | 224.12 (86.31) | 28.12 (10.83) | 259.66 (100) | 57.50 (65.56) | 25.60 (29.19) | 4.07 (4.64) | 87.17 (100) | 12.80 (40.53) | 9.40 (29.77) | 9.38 (29.70) | 31.58 (100) |
| 1995 | 165.50 (83.09) | 11.70 (5.87) | 21.97 (11.03) | 199.17 (100) | 9.28 (4.51) | 193.55 (94.13) | 2.79 (1.36) | 205.62 (100) | 88.20 (75.18) | 26.50 (22.59) | "62 (2.23) | 117.32 (1000) | 12.37 (37.29) | 12.80 (38.59) | 8.00 (24.12) | 33.17 (100) |
| 1996 | 167.20 (821.98) | 11.00 (5.39) | 25.75 (12.63) | 203.95 (100) | 9.61 (4.16) | 214.91 (93.06) | 6.41 (2.78) | 230.93 (100) | 79.20 (65.82) | 36.90 (30.67) | 4.23 (3.52) | 120.33 (100) | 12.70 (38.93) | 12.42 (38.07) | 7.50 (22.99) | 32.62 (100) |
| 1997 | 175.60 (80.98) | 13.00 (5.99) | 28.25 (13.03) | 216.85 (100) | 18.19 (7.34) | 222.78 (89.85) | 6.99 (2.82) | 247.96 (100) | 114.30 (69.46) | 43.5 (26.44) | 6.75 (4.10) | 164.55 (100) | 13.08 (41.29) | 12.40 (39.14) | 6.20 (19.57) | 31.68 (100) |
| 1998 | 148.70 (79.92) | 12.70 (6.83) | 24.65 (13.25) | 186.05 (100) | 48.03 (16.31) | 236.49 (80.28) | 10.05 (3.41) | 294.57 (100) | 126.00 (66.84) | 50.20 (26.68) | 12.30 (6.50) | 188.50 (100) | 18.10 (42.69) | 17.80 (42.98) | 6.40 (15.09) | 42.30 (100) |
| Percentage change over the period | 98.53 | 13.11 | 363.35 | 129.40 | 946.40 | 110.60 | 325.80 | 147.06 | 577.42 | 228.10 | 645.45 | 433.20 | 98.90 | 256.00 | 26.14 | 84.50 |

Note : Figures in brackets give percentage total. Source : Survey Data

**Table III. Uses of Funds**

| Year | Metal Industry | | | Machinery Industry | | | Electrical Industry | | | Transport Industry | | |
|---|---|---|---|---|---|---|---|---|---|---|---|---|
| | Current Assets | Fixed Assets | Total Assets | Current Assets | Fixed Assets | Total Assets | Current Assets | Fixed Assets | Total Assets | Current Assets | Fixed Assets | Totel Assets |
| 1988 | 83.04 (52.21) | 76.00 (47.79) | 159.04 (100) | 124.98 (88.73) | 15.87 (11.27) | 140.85 (100) | 37.20 (79.08) | 9.84 (20.92) | 47,04 (100) | 23.43 (18.85) | 100.90 (81.15) | 124.33 (100) |
| 1989 | 107.85 (56.39) | 83.42 (43.61) | 191.27 (100) | 176.99 (92.04) | 15.31 (7.96) | 192.3 (100) | 35.90 (78.56) | 9.80 (21.44) | 45.70 (100) | 21.58 (16.10) | 112.47 (83.90) | 134.05 (100) |
| 1990 | 136.70 (63.85) | 77.38 (36.15) | 214.08 (100) | 155.31 (90.50) | 16.30 (9.50) | 171.61 (100) | 38.46 (79.98) | 9.63 (20.02) | 48.09 (100) | 27.92 (18.44) | 123.45 (81.56) | 151.37 (100) |
| 1991 | 144.30 (67.67) | 68.95 (32.33) | 213.25 (100) | 177.45 (92.31) | 14.79 (7.69) | 192.24 (100) | 54.39 (85.69) | 9.08 (14.31) | 63.47 (100) | 33.92 (21.06) | 127.17 (78.94) | 161.09 (100) |
| 1992 | 160.30 (72.00) | 62.35 (28.0) | 222.65 (100) | 282.50 (95.11) | 14.51 (4.89) | 297.01 (100) | 67.40 (87.33) | 9.78 (12.67) | 77.18 (100) | 32.60 (19.63) | 133.49 (80.37) | 166.09 (100) |
| 1993 | 178.80 (75.54) | 57.89 (24.46) | 236.69 (100) | 323.24 (95.25) | 16.11 (4.75) | 339.35 (100) | 72.83 (80.42) | 17.73 (19.58) | 90.56 (100) | 34.33 (18.95) | 146.79 (81.05) | 181.12 (100) |
| 1994 | 187.20 (77.64) | 53.91 (22.36) | 241.11 (100) | 292.61 (95.12) | 15.01 (4.88) | 307.62 (100) | 89.55 (84.19) | 16.82 (15.81) | 106.37 (100) | 35.52 (18.72) | 154.2 (81.25) | 189.79 (100) |
| 1995 | 202.40 (80.40) | 49.35 (19.60) | 251.75 (100) | 245.39 (94.86) | 13.30 (5.14) | 258.69 (100) | 113.83 (86.48) | 17.79 (13.52) | 131.62 (100) | 34.14 (17.86) | 157.06 (82.14) | 191.20 (100) |
| 1996 | 207.70 (78.87) | 55.64 (21.13) | 263.34 (100) | 265.84 (94.84) | 14.45 (5.16) | 280.29 (100) | 135.78 (88.77) | 17.18 (11.23) | 152.96 (100) | 33.42 (17.47) | 157.88 (82.53) | 191.30 (100) |
| 1997 | 221.00 (80.05) | 55.09 (19.95) | 276.09 (100) | 285.53 (93.33) | 20.39 (6.67) | 305.92 (100) | 190.36 (89.23) | 22.98 (10.77) | 213.34 (100) | 34.87 (17.96) | 159.25 (82.04) | 194.12 (100) |
| 1998 | 188.60 (78.83) | 50.66 (21.17) | 239.26 (100) | 334.70 (94.03) | 21.26 (5.97) | 355.96 (100) | 192.22 (83.22) | 38.77 (16.78) | 230.99 (100) | 43.07 (20.97) | 162.32 (79.03) | 205.39 (100) |
| Percentage changes over the period. | 127.12 | 33.34 | 50.44 | 167.80 | 33.96 | 152.72 | 416.72 | 294.00 | 391.05 | 83.82 | 60.87 | 65.20 |

Note : Figures in brackets give percentage total. Source : Survey Data

## Table IV : Current Assets

| Year | Metal Industry | | | | | Machinery Insustry | | | | | Electrical Industry | | | | | Transport Industry | | | | |
|---|---|---|---|---|---|---|---|---|---|---|---|---|---|---|---|---|---|---|---|---|
| | Sundry Debtors | Closing Stock | Advance & deposits | Cash in hand& Bank | Total | Sundry Debtors | Closing Stock | Advance & Deposits | Cash in hand& Bank | Total | Sundry Debtors | Closing Stock | Advance & Deposits | Cash in hand& Bank | Total | Sundry Debtors | Closing Stock | Advance & Deposits | Cash in hand& Bank | Total |
| 1988 | 28.54 (34.37) | 10.69 (12.87) | 2.31 (2.78) | 41.50 (49.98) | 83.04 (1tOO) | 67.66 (54.14 ) | 6.37 (5.10) | 8.54 (6.83) | 42.41 (33.93) | 124.98 (100) | 23.34 (62.74) | 8.73 (23.47) | 3.78 (10.16) | 1.35 (3.63) | 37.20 (100) | 7.21 (30.77) | 11,83 (50.49) | 0.39 (1.66) | 4.00 (17.07) | 23.00 (100) |
| 1989 | 29.44 (27.30) | 14.44 (13.39) | 3.37 (3.12) | 60.60 (56.19) | 107.85 (100) | '58.52 (33.06 | 10.42 (5.89) | 9.97 (5.63) | 98.08 (55.42) | 176.99 (100) | 22.85 (63.65) | 7.72 (21.50) | 3.74 (10.42) | 1.59 (4.43) | 35.90 (100) | 6.95 (32.21) | 12.09 (56.02) | 0.18 (0.83) | 2.36 (10.94) | 21.58 (100) |
| 1990 | 30.56 (22.36) | 21.19 (15.50) | 4.39 (3.21) | 80.56 (58.93) | 136.70 (100) | 50.39 (32.44 | 8.85 (5.70) | 9.44 (6.08) | 86.63 (55.78) | 155.31 (100) | 20.54 (53.41) | 10.58 (27.51) | 5.01 (13.03) | 2.33 (6.10) | 38.46 (100) | 9.58 (34.31) | 12.83 (45.95) | 0.40 (13.43) | 5.11 (18.30) | 27.92 (100) |
| 1991 | 35.23 (24.41) | 21.81 (15.11) | 44.60 (30.91) | 42.66 (29.56) | 144.3 (100) | 25.78 (14.53 | 19.35 (10.90 | 10.71 (6.04) | 121.61 (68.53) | 177.45 (100) | 27.15 (49.92) | 20.63 (37.93) | 4.46 (8.20) | 2.15 (3.95) | 54.39 (100) | 9.96 (29.36) | 11.95 (35.23) | 0.50 (1.47) | 11.51 (33.93) | 35.52 (100) |
| 1992 | 48.05 (29.98) | 29.13 (18.17) | 43.5 (27.14) | 39.62 (24.72) | 160.30 (100) | 36.46 (12.91 | 41.65 (14.74 | 25.37 (8.98) | 179.02 (63.37) | 282.5 (100) | 34.11 (50.61) | 22.63 (33.58) | 6.79 (10.07) | 3.87 (5.74) | 67.40 (100) | 10.40 (31.90) | 12.61 (38.68) | 0.41 (1.26) | 9.18 (28.16) | 32.60 (100) |
| 1993 | 49.80 (27.86) | 38.04 (21.27) | 51.96 (29.06) | 39.00 (21.81) | 178.80 (109) | 64.50 (19.95 | 88.43 (27.36 | 30.38 (9.40) | 139.93 (43.29) | 323.24 (100) | 39.69 (54.50) | 29.38 (40.34) | 2.78 (3.82) | 0.98 (1.35) | 72.83 (100) | 10.75 (31.31) | 17.38 (50.63) | 0.22 (0.64) | 5.98 (17.42) | 34.33 (100) |
| 1994 | 69.12 (36.94) | 38.08 (20.35) | 43.40 (23.20) | 36.50 (19.51) | 187.10 (100) | 26.64 (9.10) | 41.57 (14.21 | 32.44 (11.09) | 191.95 (65.60) | 292.61 (100) | 43.09 (48.12) | 39.43 (44.03) | 5.85 (6.53) | 1.18 (1.32) | 89.55 (100) | 11.43 (32.18) | 21.26 (59.58) | 0.12 (0.34) | 2.71 (7.63) | 33.52 (100) |
| 1995 | 69.88 (34.54) | 16.86 (8.33) | 62.80 (31.04) | 52.80 (26.09) | 202.34 (100) | 15.16 (6.18) | 29.54 (12.04 | 20.97 (8.55) | 179.72 (73.24) | 245.39 (100) | 58.57 (51.45) | 45.55 (40.02) | 9.03 (7.93) | 0.68 (0.60) | 113.83 (100) | 16.96 (49.68) | 15.82 (46.34) | 0.12 (0.35) | 10.24 (3.63) | 34.14 (100) |
| 1996 | 57.26 (27.58) | 28.32 (13.64) | 76.80 (37.00) | 45.20 (21.77) | 207.58 (100) | 40.77 (15.34 | 23.45 (8.82) | 29.41 (11.06) | 172..21 (64.78) | 265.84 (100) | 67.57 (49.76) | 61.08 (44.98) | 6.46 (4.76) | 0.67 (0.49) | 135.78 (100) | 19.30 (57.75) | 10.95 (32.76) | 0.17 (0.51) | 3.00 (8.98) | 33.42 (100) |
| 1997 | 76.26 (34.51) | 42.23 (19.11) | 67.4 (30.50) | 35.10 (15.88) | 221.00 (100) | 56.37 (19.74 | 17.53 (6.14) | 16.14 (5.65) | 195.50 (68.47) | 285.53 (100) | 107.03 (56.23) | 62.34 (32.75) | 20.31 (10.67) | 0.68 (0.36) | 190.36 (100) | 18.85 (54.06) | 13.08 (37.51) | 0.28 (0.80) | 2.66 (7.63) | 34.83 (100) |
| 1998 | 75.72 (40.17) | 22.50 (11.94) | 56.0 (29.71) | 34.30 (18.19) | 188.52 (100) | 78.90 (23.57 | 30.05 (8.98) | 25.72 (7.68) | 200.03 (59.76) | 334.70 (100) | 92.71 (48.23) | 79.35 (41.28) | 19.54 (10.17) | 0.62 (0.32) | 192.22 (100) | 16.92 (39.28) | 12.09 (28.07) | 0.47 (1.09) | 13.59 (31.55) | 43.07 (100) |
| Percentage change over | 165.3 | 110.54 | 168.69 | -56.1 | 127.12 | 16.6 | 372.09 | 201.2 | 371.7 | 167.80 | 297.2 | 808.54 | 416.9 | -54.1 | 416.72 | 134.7 | 2.2 | 20.5 | 239.8 | 83.82 |

Note : Figures in brackets give percentage total. Source : Survey Data..

**Table V. Financial Ratios on Liquidity Management**

| Year | Metal Industry | | | | Machinery Insustry | | | | Electrical Industry | | | | Transport Industry | | | |
|---|---|---|---|---|---|---|---|---|---|---|---|---|---|---|---|---|
| | Metal | Machinery | Electrical | Transport | Metal | Machinery | Electrical | Transport | Metal | Machinery | Electrical | Transport | Metal | Machinery | Electrical | Transport |
| 1988 | 1.92 | 5.75 | 1.66 | 0.50 | 1.02 | 1.05 | 1.05 | 1.02 | 0.89 | 0.99 | 0.80 | 0.51 | 0.46 | 0.94 | 1.88 | 6.77 |
| 1989 | 1.16 | 12.84 | 1.45 | 0.11 | 1. 01 | 1.08 | 1.04 | 1.00 | 0.88 | 1.01 | 0.82 | 0.44 | 0.51 | 1.05 | 2.08 | 7.67 |
| 1990 | 1.51 | -0.33 | 1.93 | 0.11 | 1.01 | 0.998 | 1.05 | 1.00 | 0.85 | 0.94 | 0.76 | 0.54 | 0.68 | 1.15 | 1.84 | 6.22 |
| 1991 | 1.47 | 8.4 | 5.85 | 1.89 | 1.01 | 1.05 | 1.12 | 1.06 | 0.86 | 0.94 | 0.70 | 0.69 | 0.76 | 1.04 | 1.88 | 5.70 |
| 1992 | 1.21 | 36.79 | 3.38 | 0.14 | 1.01 | 1.15 | 1.05 | 1.00 | 0.82 | 0.98 | 0.70 | 0.62 | 0.79 | 0.72 | 1.50 | 6.70 |
| 1993 | 2.34 | 46.64 | 4.41 | 0.85 | 1.01 | 1.17 | 1.06 | 1.03 | 0.80 | 0.85 | 0.64 | 0.51 | 0.92 | 0.59 | 1.57 | 5.66 |
| 1994 | 3.00 | 32.95 | 2.38 | 3.94 | 1.02 | 1.13 | 1.03 | 1.06 | 0.81 | 0.97 | 0.57 | 0.45 | 1.03 | 1.01 | 1.60 | 12.32 |
| 1995 | 3.23 | 39.77 | -3.49 | 0.97 | 1.02 | 1.19 | 0.97 | 1.03 | 0.93 | 1.05 | 0.58 | 0.55 | 1.17 | 1.13 | 1.61 | 13.74 |
| 1996 | 3.75 | 34.91 | 14.85 | 0.80 | 1.02 | 1.15 | 1.13 | 1.02 | 0.88 | 1.05 | 0.62 | 0.69 | 0.97 | 1.14 | 2.20 | 14.57 |
| 1997 | 4.15 | 37.57 | 25.81 | 3.29 | 1.02 | 1.15 | 1.16 | 1.10 | 0.82 | 1.08 | 0.78 | 0.69 | 1.20 | 1.33 | 1.54 | 12.98 |
| 1998 | 2.55 | 40.13 | 3.72 | 0.77 | 1.01 | 1.14 | 1.02 | 1.02 | 0.89 | 1.03 | 0.60 | 0.73 | 2.15 | 1.38 | 1.25 | 14.38 |

Source : Survey Data.

**Table VI- financial Ratios on Inventory Management and Cash Management**

| Year | Ratio of Inventory to Current assets | | | | Ratio of Current Assets | | | | Working Capital turnover ratio | | | |
|---|---|---|---|---|---|---|---|---|---|---|---|---|
| | Metal | Machinery | Electrical | Transport | Metal | Machinery | Electrical | Transport | Metal | Machinery | Electrical | Transport |
| 1988 | 0.13 | 0.05 | 0.23 | 0.50 | 0.51 | 0.34 | 0.04 | 0.17 | 19.92 | 20.53 | 42.04 | 317.40 |
| 1989 | 0.13 | 0.06 | 0.22 | 0.59 | 0.56 | 0.55 | 0.04 | 0.11 | 47.84 | 21.52 | 51.44 | 1505.00 |
| 1990 | 0.16 | 0.06 | 0.28 | 0.46 | 0.59 | 0.56 | 0.06 | 0.18 | 61.23 | - | 36.60 | 1577.82 |
| 1991 | 0.15 | 0.44 | 0.38 | 0.35 | 0.30 | 0.69 | 0.04 | 0.34 | 75.04 | 22.06 | 17.45 | 102.34 |
| 1992 | 0.18 | 0.15 | 0.34 | 0.39 | 0.25 | 0.63 | 0.06 | 0.28 | 105.2 | 5.53 | 29.84 | 1559.14 |
| 1993 | 0.21 | 0.27 | 0.40 | 0.51 | 0.22 | 0.43 | 0.01 | 0.17 | 70.00 | 4.06 | 25.87 | 228.73 |
| 1994 | 0.20 | 0.14 | 0.44 | 0.63 | 0.19 | 0.66 | 0.01 | 0.08 | 64.36 | 8.98 | 56.66 | 104.83 |
| 1995 | 0.08 | 0.12 | 0.40 | 0.46 | 0.26 | 0.73 | 0.01 | 0.04 | 73.47 | 7.00 | - | 483.47 |
| 1996 | 0.14 | 0.09 | 0.45 | 0.33 | 0.22 | 0.65 | neg | 0.09 | 53.72 | 9.80 | 20.11 | 608.48 |
| 1997 | 0.19 | 0.06 | 0.33 | 0.38 | 0.16 | 0.68 | neg | 0.08 | 63.81 | 10.08 | 11.37 | 137.57 |
| 1998 | 0.12 | 0.09 | 0.41 | 0.28 | 0.18 | 0.60 | neg | 0.32 | 159.2 | 11.51 | 64.66 | 804.30 |

Source : Survey Data.

**Table VII. Financial Ratios Indicating Financial Strength**

| Year | Operational Performance | | | | | | | | Assets Utilisation | | | | | | | |
|---|---|---|---|---|---|---|---|---|---|---|---|---|---|---|---|---|
| | Gross Profit Ratio | | | | Operating Ratio | | | | Assets Turnover Ratio | | | | Net Fixed Capital Turnover Ratio | | | |
| | Metal | Machinery | Electrical | Transport | Metal | Machinery | Electrical | Transport | Metal | Machinery | Electrical | Transport | Metal | Machinery | Electrical | Transport |
| 1988 | 0.24 | 0.17 | 0.34 | 0.26 | 0.7 | 0.83 | 0.73 | 0.74 | 0.24 | 0.84 | 1.48 | 1.28 | 0.50 | 7.44 | 7.00 | 1.57 |
| 1989 | 0.45 | 0.13 | 0.21 | 0.19 | 0.5 | 0.87 | 0.79 | 0.81 | 0.28 | 0.97 | 1.63 | 1.23 | 0.67 | 12.17 | 7.61 | 1.47 |
| 1990 | 0.33 | 0.13 | 0.31 | 0.19 | 0.6 | 0.87 | 0.69 | 0.81 | 0.43 | 1.04 | 1.47 | 1.15 | 1.19 | 10.94 | 7.34 | 1.41 |
| 1991 | 0.27 | 0.24 | 0.18 | 0.11 | 0.7 | 0.76. | 0.82 | 0.89 | 0.52 | 0.96 | 1.61 | 1.20 | 1.60 | 12.53 | 11.24 | 1.52 |
| 1992 | 0.03 | 0.20 | 0.12 | 0.20 | 0.9 | 0.80 | 0.88 | 0.80 | 0.57 | 0.69 | 1.31 | 1.31 | 2.04 | 14.03 | 10.31 | 1.64 |
| 1993 | 0.10 | 0.23 | 0.05 | 0.25 | 0.9 | 0.77 | 0.95 | 0.75 | 0.69 | 0.56 | 1.26 | 1.07 | 2.83 | 11.76 | 6.43 | 1.32 |
| 1994 | 0.14 | 0.16 | 0.17 | 0.28 | 0.8 | 0.84 | 0.83 | 0.71 | 0.80 | 0.96 | 1.33 | 2.18 | 3.58 | 19.71 | 8.44 | 2.68 |
| 1995 | 0.07 | 0.11 | 0.27 | 0.26 | 0.9 | 0.90 | 0.73 | 0.74 | 0.94 | 1.08 | 1.39 | 2.45 | 4.81 | 20.92 | 10.28 | 2.99 |
| 1996 | 0.06 | 0.10 | 0.23 | 0.20 | 0.9 | 0.89 | 0.77 | 0.80 | 0.77 | 1.08 | 1.95 | 2.54 | 3.62 | 20.90 | 17.38 | 3.08 |
| 1997 | 0.17 | 0.13 | neg | 0.19 | 0.8 | 0.87 | 0.93 | 0.81 | 0.96 | 1.24 | 1.38 | 2.33 | 4.81 | 18.57 | 12.78 | 2.84 |
| 1998 | 0.18 | 0.08 | 0.15 | 0.13 | 0.8 | 0.92 | 0.85 | 0.87 | 1.70 | 1.30 | 1.04 | 3.02 | 8.01 | 21.72 | 6.20 | 3.82 |

Source : Survey Data.

**Table VIII. Bifurcated Operating Ratio**

| rear | Raw Material & Fuel Cost to | | | | Salaries & Wages to Sales | | | | Other Establishment Cost to Sales | | | |
|---|---|---|---|---|---|---|---|---|---|---|---|---|
| | Metal | Machinery | Electrical | Transport | Metal | Machinery | Electrical | Transport | Metal | Machinery | Electrical | Transport |
| 1988 | 0.38 | 0.62 | 0.52 | 0.59 | 0.18 | 0.11 | 0.19 | 0.03 | 0.15 | 0.11 | 0.01 | 0.05 |
| 1989 | 0.25 | 0.67 | 0.61 | 0.65 | 0.15 | 0.07 | 0.17 | 0.05 | 0.12 | 0.12 | 0.01 . | 0.05 |
| 1990 | 0.43 | 0.73 | 0.49 | 0.63 | 0.13 | 0.08 | 0.19 | 0.05 | 0.8 | 0.06 | 0.01 | 0.05 |
| 1991 | 0.58 | 0.57 | 0.54 | 0.71 | 0.16 | 0.08 | 0.19 | 0.06 | 0.7 | 0.11 | 0.02 | 0.05 |
| 1992 | 0.72 | 0.57 | 0.63 | 0.63 | 0.15 | 0.08 | 0.23 | 0.05 | 0.6 | 0.14 | 0.02 | 0.05 |
| 1993 | 0.65 | 0.48 | 0.74 | 0.61 | 0.16 | 0.09 | 0.19 | 0.03 | 0.6 | 0.20 | 0.02 | 0.05 |
| 1994 | 0.63 | 0.67 | 0.61 | 0.61 | 0.13 | 0.06 | 0.19 | 0.03 | 0.7 | 0.11 | 0.03 | 0.03 |
| 1995 | 0.67 | 0.70 | 0.59 | 0.62 | 0.16 | 0.09 | 0.12 | 0.03 | 0.8 | 0.10 | 0.02 | 0.04 |
| 1996 | 0.66 | 0.68 | 0.62 | 0.66 | 0.17 | O.O'I | 0.13 | 0.05 | 0.7 | 0.12 | 0.01 | 0.04 |
| 1997 | 0.52 | 0.48 | 0.79 | 0.67 | 0.19 | 0.12 | 0.19 | 0.06 | 0.9 | 0.27 | 0.02 | 0.06 |
| 1998 | 0.56 | 0.53 | 0.71 | 0.70 | 0.17 | 0.10 | 0.12 | 0.03 | 0.8 | 0.29 | 0.02 | 0.06 |

Source : Survey Data.

**Table IX. Financial Ratios of Different Engineering Croups at all India**

| Year | Current ratio | | | | Gross profit (Percent) | | | | Assets turnover ratio (times) | | | | Net fixed capital turnover ratio (times) | | | | Working capital turnover ratio (times) | | | |
|---|---|---|---|---|---|---|---|---|---|---|---|---|---|---|---|---|---|---|---|---|
| | Metal | Mach inery | Electr ical | Trans port | Metal | Mach inery | Electr ical | Trans port | Metal | Mach inery | Electr ical | Trans port | Metal | Mach inery | Electr ical | Trans port | Metal | Mach inery | Electr ical | Trans port |
| 1990-91 | 1.24 | 1.34 | 1.36 | 1.34 | 14.9 | 11.7 | 9.9 | 10.90 | 0.61 | 0.95 | 0.99 | 0.92 | 1.0 | 3.0 | 2.89 | 2.10 | 0.91 | 2.29 | 2.53 | 2.11 |
| 1991-92 | 1.13 | 1.34 | 1.36 | 1.31 | 15.5 | 12.9 | 10.9 | 11.00 | 0.64 | 0.93 | 0.96 | 0.95 | 1.05 | 2.53 | 2.69 | 2.01 | 0.96 | 2.30 | 2.54 | 2.27 |
| 1992-93 | 1.04 | 1.37 | 1.39 | 1.28 | 14.3 | 13.3 | 12.1 | 10.70 | 0.61 | 0.93 | 0.94 | 0.94 | 1.02 | 2.51 | 2.62 | 1.97 | 0.96 | 2.22 | 2.34 | 2.21 |
| 1993-94 | 1.30 | 1.39 | 1.42 | 1.18 | 13.5 | 13.8 | 11.9 | 12.60 | 0.57 | 0.91 | 0.95 | 0.97 | 0.94 | 2.41 | 2.55 | 2.06 | 0.91 | 2.07 | 2.22 | 2.38 |
| 1994-95 | 1.30 | 1.40 | 1.42 | 1.16 | 16.3 | 13.0 | 11.8 | 13.30 | 0.61 | 0.93 | 0.96 | 0.04 | 0.99 | 2.45 | 2.66 | 2.34 | 0.93 | 2.00 | 2.11 | 2.70 |
| 1995-96 | 1.20 | 1.34 | 1.40 | 1.10 | 17.5 | 12.5 | 11.6 | 14.20 | 0.62 | 0.96 | 0.97 | 1.09 | 1.04 | 2.54 | 2.68 | 2.60 | 0.95 | 2.01 | 2.08 | 2.86 |
| 1996-97 | 1.20 | 1.34 | 1.35 | 1.30 | 15.4 | 13.0 | 12.5 | 14.00 | 0.58 | 0.92 | 0.92 | 1.06 | 0.95 | 2.34 | 2.36 | 2.52 | 0.89 | 1.94 | 2.00 | 2.45 |
| 1997-98 | 1.20 | 1.34 | 1.32 | 1.25 | 14.3 | 12.3 | 11.2 | 14.10 | 0.54 | 0.91 | 0.86 | 0.88 | 0.86 | 2.17 | 2.01 | 2.09 | 0.84 | 1.86 | 1.84 | 1.83 |

Source : Compiled from Financial Aggregates & Katios, Centre for Monitoring Indian Economy (CMIE)

Note : Information relating to financial ratios prior to 1990-91 were not available.

## Table X: Classification of Groups Based on the Values of Different Industrial Ratios

| *Sl. No.* | *Industrial Ratios* | *Favourable Zone (Healthy Zone)* | *Unfavourable Zone (Bankrupt Zone)* | *Grey Zone (Range between Favourable & Unfavourable Zone)* |
|---|---|---|---|---|
| X1 | Working Capital to Total assets ratio | Above 30 % | Below 15 % | Between 15 % and 30 % |
| X3 | Gross Profit (EBIT) to Total Assets ratio | Above 10 % | Zero or below | Between zero and 10 % |
| X4 | Net Worth to Total Liabilities Ratio | Above 100 % | Below 50 % | Between 50 % and 100 % |
| X5 | Sales to Total Assets | Above 100 % | Below 50 % | Between 50 % and 100 % |

**Table XI Industrial Ratios of the Engineering Groups Based on Altman's Model**

| Year | Metal product group | | | | Machinery Group | | | | Electrical Group | | | | Transport Group | | | |
|---|---|---|---|---|---|---|---|---|---|---|---|---|---|---|---|---|
| | Working capital to total assets | Gross profit to total assets ratio | Net worth to total liabilities ratio | Sales to total assets ratio | Working capital to total assets | Gross profit to total assets ratio | Net worth to total liabilities ratio | Sales to total assets ratio | Working capital to total assets | Gross profit to total assets | Net worth to total liabilities ratio | Sales to total assets ratio | Working capital to total assets | Gross profit to total assets | Net worth to total liabilities ratio | Sales to total assets ratio |
| 1988 | 0.01 | 0.06 | 0.49 | 0.24 | 0.04 | 0.14 | 0.15 | 0.84 | 0.04 | 0.50 | 0.24 | 1.48 | 0 | 0.33 | 0.82 | 1.28 |
| 1989 | 0.01 | 0.13 | 0.47 | 0.28 | 0.07 | 0.13 | 0.15 | 0.97 | 0.03 | 0.35 | 0.25 | 1.63 | 0 | 0.23 | 0.84 | 1.23 |
| 1990 | 0.01 | 0.14 | 0.37 | 0.43 | 0 | 0.13 | 0.09 | 1.04 | 0.04 | 0.46 | 0.24 | 1.47 | 0 | 0.22 | 0.82 | 1.15 |
| 1991 | 0.01 | 0.14 | 0.33 | 0.52 | 0.04 | 0.23 | 0.12 | 0.96 | 0.09 | 0.29 | 0.24 | 1.61 | 0.01 | 0.14 | 0.80 | 1.20 |
| 1992 | 0.01 | 0.02 | 0.28 | 0.57 | 0.12 | 0.14 | 0.17 | 0.69 | 0.04 | 0.16 | 0.17 | 1.31 | 0 | 0.27 | 0.81 | 1.31 |
| 1993 | 0.01 | 0.07 | 0.25 | 0.69 | 0.14 | 0.13 | 0.19 | 0.56 | 0.05 | 0.06 | 0.24 | 1.26 | 0 | 0.27 | 0.82 | 1.07 |
| 1994 | 0.01 | 0.12 | 0.24 | 0.80 | 0.11 | 0.16 | 0.16 | 0.96 | 0.02 | 0.23 | 0.18 | 1.33 | 0.02 | 0.62 | 0.83 | 2.18 |
| 1995 | 0.01 | 0.07 | 0.21 | 0.94 | 0.15 | 0.11 | 0.21 | 1.08 | -0.03 | 0.38 | 0.11 | 1.39 | 0.01 | 0.63 | 0.83 | 2.45 |
| 1996 | 0.01 | 0.05 | 0.23 | 0.77 | 0.12 | 0.11 | 0.18 | 1.08 | 0.10 | 0.45 | 0.12 | 1.95 | 0 | 0.51 | 0.83 | 2.54 |
| 1997 | 0.02 | 0.17 | 0.21 | 0.96 | 0.12 | 0.16 | 0.19 | 1.24 | 0.12 | 0.01 | 0.23 | 1.38 | 0.02 | 0.44 | 0.84 | 2.33 |
| 1998 | 0.01 | 0.31 | 0.22 | 1.70 | 0.11 | 0.11 | 0.17 | 1.30 | 0.02 | 0.16 | 0.18 | 1.04 | 0 | 0.40 | 0.79 | 3.02 |

Source : Computed from Survey Data.

## Table XII: 'Z' Score

| *Year* | *Metal Products Group* | *Machinery Group* | *Electrical Group* | *Transport Group* |
|---|---|---|---|---|
| 1989 | 0.76 | 1.48 | 3.40 | 2.93 |
| 1989 | 1.01 | 1.62 | 3.05 | 2.55 |
| 1990 | 1.15 | 1.58 | 3.25 | 2.43 |
| 1991 | 1.22 | 1.89 | 2.90 | 2.21 |
| 1992 | 0.84 | 1.43 | 2.05 | 2.75 |
| 1993 | 1.12 | 1.30 | 1.73 | 2.51 |
| 1994 | 1.39 | 1.76 | 2.29 | 4.86 |
| 1995 | 1.36 | 1.8 | 2.74 | 5.16 |
| 1996 | 1.12 | 1.75 | 3.72 | 4.85 |
| 1997 | 1.72 | 2.08 | 1.76 | 4.43 |
| 1998 | 2.95 | 1.96 | 1.75 | 4.97 |

*Source:* Computed from Survey Data.

# *Bibliography*


Agarwal RN & BN Goldar (1999). Technical imports growth, efficiency and export performance of Indian engineering firms in the prc and post reform period. Institute of Economic Growth. Working Paper, Series No. E/201/99. Delhi University Enclave, Delhi.

Ahluwalia, I.J, (1985), *Industrial Growth in India—Stagnation since mid sixties,* Oxford University Press, New Delhi.

——, (1991), *Productivity and Growth in Indian Industries,* Oxford University Press, New Delhi.

——, (1990): 'Recent Technology Imports into India: Results of a Survey', *Development and Change,* Vol XXI, pp. 723-49.

——, (1990): *Technological Advance in the Third World,* Zed Books, London.

——(1990):, 'Import of Technology and the Technological Effort of Indian Enterprises', *World Development,* Vol. 18, No. 3.

—— (1992): 'Technological Change and Restructuring in Asian Industries: Implications for Human Resources Development' in M. Muqtada and A. Hildeman (eds.), *Labour Markets and Human Resource Planning in Asia: Perspectives and Evidence,* UNDP and ARTEP/ILC, Geneva and New Delhi.

—— (1993b): 'SAP and Education: Issues Related to Equity', mimeo. Institute for Social and Economic Change, Bangalore.

Alam, G. (1993): 'Research and Development by Indian Industry: A Study of the Determinants of its Size and Scope', mimeo, Centre for Technology Studies, New Delhi.

Altman, E.I. (1968), "Financial Ratios. Discriminant Analysis and prediction of corporate bankruptcy". *Journal of Finance,* Vol. XIII. Sept., pp. 589-609.

Anker, R. (ed.) (1982), *Interaction Between Women's Roles and Population Trends in the Third World,* CroomHelm : London.

Arshad, M. Khan and Veerachai Memopichotorattana. (1985), "Predicting business failure : Models and judgement", *The Chartered Accountant,* Vol. XXXIV. October, p. 298.

Bardhan, P. (1984): *The Political Economy of Development in India,* Basil Blackwell, Oxford.

Bhagavan, M.R. (1987): 'A Critique of India's Economic Policies and Strategies', *Monthly Review,* Vol. 39, No 3, July-August.

Buvinic et al. (ed.) (1983), *Women and Poverty in the Third World,* The John Hopkins University Press, Baltimore.

Das, T.K. (1993): 'Structural Reforms and Stabilisation Policies in India: Rationale and Medium-Term Outlook' in Gupta, 1993.

Department of Scientific and Industrial Research, Government of India.

Desai, A.V. (1988): *Technology Absorption in Indian Industry*, Wiley Eastern, New Delhi.

Dyson, T. & M. Moor (1983), "On Kinship Structure, Female Autonomy and Demographic Behaviour in India", *Population and Development Review*, 9 : 35-60

Erich, A. Gekfert, Richard D. Irwin. (1957) *Techniques of Financial Analysis*, Homewood, p. 257.

*Far Eastern Economic Review* (1992): "Time to Catch Up: India Tries to Bring Science Closer to Business", December 10, pp. 45-46.

Freeman, C. (1982): *The Economics of Industrial Innovation*, Second Edition, Francis Pinter, England.

Ghose, A.K. (1993): "Employment in Organised Manufacturing in India", mimeo, ARTEP/ ILO, New Delhi.

*Guardian Weekly* (1994): "Last Words Go to, People and Jobs", July 3, p. 5.

Gumaste, V. (1988): "Anatomy of In-House R and D: A Case Study of Indian Automobile Industry", *Economic and Political Weekly*, Vol XXIII, Review of Management, pp. M 67-72.

Gupta, S.P. (ed.) (1993): *Liberalisation: Its Impact on the Indian Economy*, Macmillan, Delhi.

ILO-ARTEP (1992): *Social Dimensions of Structural Adjustment in India*, New Delhi.

India-DST(1992): Annual Register of Foreign Collaborations, 1992 and preceding issues.

India-DST (1992): Research and Development Statistics, 1990-91 and preceding years, Department of Science and Technology, Government of India.

Jacob, Jojo (1999). Technology behaviour and Export performance: A firm level analysis of Indian Electrical Machine Industry, M.Phil. Dissertation, CDS, Trivandrum.

Jejeebhoy (1995), *Women's Education, Autonomy and Reproductive Behaviour : Experience from Developiong Countries,* Clarendon : Oxford.

Jones, G.W. (1977), "The Economic and Social Supports for High Fertility : Conceptual Framework", in : Ruzickal (ed.). *The Economic and Social Supports for High Fertility,* Canberra, pp. 3-39.

Kathuria, S. (1989): "Market Structure and Innovation", *Economic and Political Weekly,* August 26.

Katrak, H. (1989): "Imported Technologies and R and D in a Newly Industrialising Country: The Experience of Indian Enterprises", *Journal of Development Economics,* Vol. 31, July.

Keegan, W. (1993): *The Spectre of Capitalism: The Future of the World Economy after the Fall of Communism,* Radius, England.

Kumar Mahadevan (1981), "Engineering Export : Exports from Southern region", *Commerce,* December 26, pp. 35-36.

Lajipathi Rai, H. and Janardana Shastri (1989), "India in World Engineering Exports", *Southern Economist,* October, p. 20.

Kumar, N (1987): "Technology Imports and Local Research and Development in Indian Manufacturing", *The Developing Economies*, September.

Kurien, C.T. (1986): "Caught in Contradictions of Mixed Economy", *Economic and Political Weekly*, April 12.

Lall, S. (1987): *Learning to Industrialise: The Acquisition of Technological Capability by India*, Macmillan. Basingstoke.

Lall, S. (1990): Building Industrial Competitiveness in Developing Countries, OECD Development Centre. Paris.

Lane, R.E. (1993): *The Market Experience*, Cambridge.

Lipietz, A. (1993): *Towards a New Economic Order: Post-Fordism, Ecology and Democracy*, Polity Press, England.

Mahalanobis, P. C. (1955). "The general approach to the Plan Frame" in Bose, P.K., M. Mukherjee (ed), *Papers on Planning*, Statistical Publishing Society, Calcutta, pp. 71-82.

Majumdar, A.G., (1962), *The Indian Engineering Industry, Trends and Prospects*, Economic and Scientific Research Foundation, Federation House, New Delhi.

Miller, Donald L., (1966), *The Meaningful Interpretation of Financial Statement*, American Management Association, New York, p. 24.

Munmohun & S.N. Goyal, (1973). *Principles of Management Accounting*, Sahitya Bhavan, Agra, p. 12.

Metcalf, R.W. and Titard, P.L. (1976), *Principles of* Accounting, W.B. Saunders, Philadelphia, p. 56

Nayyar, D (1993): "Indian Economy at the Cross Roads: Illusions and Realities", *Economic and Political Weekly,* April 10.

Nelson, R.R. (1993): *National Innovation Systems: A Comparative Analysis,* Oxford University Press, New York.

Palibandala, M. (1988), "Firm size and Export behaviour: A study of the Indian Engineering Industry", Discussion paper No. 45, ICRIER, New Delhi.

Pandey, I.M. (1986), *Management Accounting,* Vikas Publishing House, New Delhi, p. 89.

Patnaik, P(1986): "New Turn in Economic Policy: Contexts and Prospects—", *Economic and Political Weekly,* June 7.

Piper (20(X)), "De-Industrialisation in developing countries : Cross country evidence on productivity and employment—", *The Journal of Development Studies,* 36 (4).

Raghuram, S. (ed) (1992): *Development Policy: Issues and Challenges for the 90s,* HIVOS, Bangalore.

Sada Shankar (1990), *Thrust Sectors in Indian Exports,* Commonwealth Publishers, New Delhi.

Saha, Surajit K. (1993). "Uneven Development of engineering companies in India—Spatial dimension of competitve advantage," *Economic & Political Weekly,* Nov. 27, p. Ml22-135.

Sandesara, J.C. (1992): *Industrial Policy and Planning 1947-91,* Sage Publications, New Delhi.

Sanjaya Lal & Rajiv Kumar (1981), "Firm level export performance in an inward looking economy : The Indian Engineering Industry", *World Development,* Vol. 9, No. 5. pp. 453-486.

Sau, Ranjit K. (1970). "Rate of Return in Engineering Industry", *Economic & Political Weekly,* Vol. 5, No. 9, February, p. M39.

Shatrugna, M. (1993): "Education, Equity and Privatisation", mimeo, Seminar paper presented at the Institute of Public Enterprise, Hyderabad.

Sigurdson, J. (1990): "The Internationalisation of R and D: An Interpretation of Forces and Responses" in J. Sigurdson (ed). *Measuring the Dynamics of Technological Change,* Francis Pinter, London.

Sukla, R.C. and T.S. Grewal, *Advance Accounts*, Sultan Chand & Company Ltd., New Delhi.

Suvrathan, P.I. (1991), "Machine Tool Industry— Export performance and prospects", *Economic & Political Weekly,* Feb. 23, pp. M 13-M 20.

Swaminathan, P. (1997), "Work and Reproductive Health : A Hobson's Choice of Indian Women", *EPW* pp. Ws 53-Ws61.

Trehan. Dinesh (1970), "Exports of Engineering goods— Recent Boom and its causes", *Economic & Political Weekly,* July, Vol V, No 27, pp. 53-57,

Tyabji, N. (1993): "Technological Collaborations and Partial Absorption: The Failure of Indian Industry in the 1980s", mimeo, Madras Institute of Development Studies, Madras.

Upendranath, C. (1993a): "Political Economy of Education in India", mimeo, Institute for Social and Economic Change, Bangalore.

Usha Kumary, K., (1992). A Study of the linkages of electrical machinery industry in Kerala. PhD dissertation, Cochin University of Science and Technology (CUSAT), Cochin.

Vyasulu, V. (1993): "The New Economic Policy and Technological Change: Towards New Initiatives", mimeo, Institute of Public Enterprise, Hyderabad.

World Bank (1993): The East Asian Miracle: Economic Growth and Public Policy, Washington, DC.

*World Development* (1994): Special Section edited by Alice H. Amsden, Vol. 22, No. 4, April.